RELATIONAL DIPLOMACY

INNOVATIONS IN PEACEBUILDING: A CASE STUDY OF CYPRUS

DAVID SANTULLI

ISBN: 0983285209
ISBN-13: 9780983285205

"Extend a hand whether or not you know it shall be grasped."

- Ryunosuke Satoro

CONTENTS

PREFACE

Relationships are the building blocks of a united planet. A united planet provides the platform of cooperation, mutual respect, and understanding needed to overcome the challenges of today's world and reach our fullest potential as a global community. We are all relational diplomats. Each and every one of us has the power to strengthen the web of human relationships and thereby create a better world. Whether you are a specialist in conflict resolution, a non-profit professional, a neighbor holding a door, or a stranger sharing a smile, every gesture that we make—no matter how small—creates ripples of goodwill throughout humanity. When stigmas and mistrust blind us and blur our vision, we need first movers who recognize our common humanity and reach out to the other side at their own peril and against the ridicule of their own governments and peers. In Cyprus, it has been these first movers, these relational diplomats, from both sides of the infamous green line, who created a citizens movement that eventually led to the opening of the borders. By employing innovative peacebuilding techniques and utilizing technology, these peacebuilders reframed the conflict and planted seeds of peace among the citizens of Cyprus. In a world grown weary of conflict, the lessons and innovations gleaned from the peacebuilders of this small island state provide valuable clues for other parts of the world. After all, what unites us is far greater than what tears us apart. It is upon this that we must focus.

David Santulli

AUTHOR'S NOTE

The case study of this book examines the developments in relational diplomacy in Cyprus from the introduction of the Internet on the island in 1995 to the surprise border opening of April 23, 2003. The innovative peacebuilding strategies and applications of technology born out of the necessity of these times provide essential clues for peacebuilders in other parts of the world.

INTRODUCTION

"We must combine the toughness of the serpent and the softness of the dove, a tough mind and a tender heart."
-- *Martin Luther King, Jr.*

Peace leader, Nicos Anastasiou, always shares this quote in his inspirational and informational email newsletters sent periodically to over 7,000 friends of Cyprus around the world on both sides of the conflict.

Cyprus has been divided since 1974 when Turkey invaded the north in response to a Greek Cypriot military coup backed by the Athens government seeking immediate *enosis* or "union with Greece." During the invasion, Turkish troops took over the northern third of the island and there were thousands of casualties and explicit reports of atrocities, including torture and multiple rapes. Additionally, over 200,000 Greek and Turkish Cypriots were forced to flee their homes. Since 1974, there have been many failed attempts at official diplomacy and occasional surges in intercommunal violence. Painful memories, confused by cultural, religious, linguistic, and ideological differences, have contributed to the prolongation of this seemingly intractable conflict. On April 23, 2003, Turkish Cypriots, prompted by a massive citizens movement, rekindled the embers of hope in a surprise move to reopen the border.

In the early 1990s, third party actors, including Conflict Resolution NGOs, began to intervene in the peacebuilding process. These efforts helped spawn a proliferation of bicommunal citizen diplomacy in the late 90s and beyond which led up to the border reopening. Third party actors have utilized a diverse range of peacebuilding tools to adapt to the ever-changing conflictual environment in Cyprus.

Confronted by the enforced division and limited communication access, some of these peacebuilders have effectively and innovatively utilized technology to greatly enhance their peacebuilding efforts. These note-worthy technological innovations deserve closer examination, particularly given the lack of research in the burgeoning area of technologically empowered peacebuilding.

The purpose of this book is: to explore the evolution of the use of technology in the peacebuilding efforts in Cyprus; to examine the particular roles and applications of technology in peacebuilding, along with inherent limitations; to consider pertinent theoretical implications from a range of disciplines; and ultimately to shed light upon the valuable role of technology as a viable tool to complement and empower the efforts of third party peacebuilders. Along the way, I will share insights from in-depth interviews with Track II practitioners, academics, and citizen peacebuilders and also introduce the concept of relational diplomacy as a peacebuilding strategy. The focus of this book will be on peacebuilding by non-state actors, not official macro-level diplomacy by states.

BACKGROUND

From 1974 until April 23, 2003, no free movement, communications, or other contacts were allowed among the Greek and Turkish Cypriots. Greek and Turkish Cypriots have lived and developed separately in two distinct geographical zones.[1] The relaxation of border controls on April 23, 2003 represents a monumental breakthrough in official relations. While the political situation remained deadlocked for decades, unofficial diplomacy has played a key role in transforming relationships and influencing public and political opinion.

Unofficial (Citizen's or Track II) diplomacy refers to informal interactions among influential members of conflicting groups aimed at developing strategies to influence public opinion and organize resources (both manpower and material) in ways favorable to the peaceful resolution of the conflict.[2]

This section provides a brief historical background of the primary unofficial peacebuilding efforts in Cyprus. An understanding of these earlier events will provide some insights into why technological interventions have played such an important role in the peacebuilding process in later years.

Benjamin J. Broome, the first resident Fulbright Scholar in conflict resolution in Cyprus, outlines five phases to the development of conflict resolution activities in Cyprus (see also Appendix A).[3] According to Broome's model, each phase laid the groundwork for the subsequent phases. The first

---

1   Maria Hadjipavlou-Trigeorgis, "Unofficial Inter-Communal Contacts and Their Contribution to Peacebuilding in Conflict Societies: The Case of Cyprus," in *The Cyprus Review,* Volume 5, Number 2, Fall 1993, p. 73.
2   Ibid., p. 69.
3   Benjamin J. Broome, "Overview of Conflict Resolution Activities in Cyprus: Their Contribution to the Peace Process," *The Cyprus Review,*, 1997, pp. 48-54.

phase of conflict resolution activities dealing with the Cyprus conflict started in 1966, when John Burton and his colleagues in London offered a five-day workshop in "controlled communication" that brought together high-level representatives from the two communities. Other programs included problem-solving workshops conducted by Herbert Kelman in 1979 and 1984.[4]

The second phase began with a local initiative of intercommunal contacts that started in September 1989, and led to the formation of the "Greek Cypriot and Turkish Cypriot Citizen's Movement for Democracy and Federation in Cyprus." The Peace Center was also formed in the Greek Cypriot community during this time.[5]

The third phase began in July 1991, when Louise Diamond, a conflict resolution specialist from the Institute for Multi-Track Diplomacy (IMTD) was invited to Cyprus at the invitation of members of the newly formed Peace Center. Dr. Diamond explored the need for training in conflict resolution and various parties began to conduct conflict resolution training around this time. In 1994, the Cyprus Fulbright Commission (CFC), directed by Daniel Hadjittofi, organized several conflict resolution training programs, which were conducted by the Cyprus Consortium, a partnership among IMTD, the Conflict Management Group (led by Diana Chigas), and the National Training Laboratory (NTL) in Virginia.[6] During this initial phase, the Cyprus Consortium trained over 400 people in six months.[7] Many of these initial trainees included peacebuilders who then made significant contributions in later years, in areas including technology based initiatives: Yiannis Laouris, Harry Anastasiou, and Nicos Anastasiou.[8] These bicommunal conflict resolution training programs were sometimes interrupted by intermittent border closings and visa denials, particularly on the Turkish Cypriot side. In 1994, Denktas closed the borders and bicommunal groups were forced to meet in the buffer zone at the UN Ledra Palace Hotel Headquarters. Later, during the period 1995-1997,

---

4   Ibid.
5   Ibid.
6   Ibid.
7   Interview with Professor Diana Chigas on May 9, 2003.
8   Ibid.

the Cyprus Consortium in both Cyprus and the United States, conducted more workshops, including an advanced training of trainers' workshop.[9]

The fourth phase had its beginnings in 1994, with the establishment of the resident Fulbright Scholar position in conflict resolution. Both local initiators and Daniel Hadjittofi at the Fulbright Commission saw the need for an outside third-party expert in conflict resolution who could be in full-time residence over an extended period in order to offer ongoing training and to help facilitate bicommunal contacts.[10]

It should also be noted that the US government, through USAID, created a $15 million dollar fund to support conflict resolution efforts. The Fulbright commission has sponsored many Greek and Turkish Cypriot scholars to study in the US. This funding, in part, has allowed Cyprus to achieve the third highest level of education in the world.[11] Several Fulbright Scholars have played an important role in the building of technological peace initiatives.

Between October 1994 and June 1995, a series of workshops was held for a core group of participants who called themselves the "Conflict Resolution Trainers," or simply "Trainers." This group utilized a problem-solving and design process referred to as Interactive Management (IM). These design sessions focused on the development of a peacebuilding strategy for Cyprus. The most crucial results of this workshop included: a systems analysis of the obstacles to peacebuilding in Cyprus; a bicommunal "collective vision statement" for the future of peacebuilding; a 2-3 year plan of activities, which included 242 separate possibilities for workshops, presentations, training programs, and other events that could make a difference in Cyprus.[12]

Out of these 242 activities, the group selected 15 projects for immediate implementation, organized an activities fair, called the agora or bazaar, and began recruiting interested participants. According to Broome, this 1995 agora/bazaar led to a major turning point for conflict resolution work

---

9   Benjamin J. Broome, "Overview of Conflict Resolution Activities in Cyprus: Their Contribution to the Peace Process", *The Cyprus Review*, 1997, pp. 48-54.

10   Ibid.

11   Interview with Professor Diana Chigas on May 9, 2003.

12   Benjamin J. Broome, "Overview of Conflict Resolution Activities in Cyprus: Their Contribution to the Peace Process", *The Cyprus Review*, 1997, pp. 48-54.

in Cyprus and marked the fifth stage in the evolution of conflict resolution activities on the island.[13]

This fifth stage was characterized by a significant expansion of peacebuilding activities among Cypriots. Guided by their vision statement and the set of 15 projects, the core group of conflict resolution trainers formed new groups with young business leaders, young political leaders, educators, students, women, and various assemblies of citizens. Special events such as concerts, poetry evenings, and other cultural activities were held. By 1997, more than 1500 Cypriots were involved in various bicommunal groups and projects.[14]

In 1997, with the Greek application for accession into the European Union, tensions were on the rise. Turkish Cypriots were harassed for taking part in the bicommunal activities and civil servants were prohibited from participating. Just as the momentum started to build for these peacebuilding efforts, Denktas cut off all access at the border, except in the bicommunal village of Pyla.[15] Greek Cypriot and peacebuilder, Dr. Laouris, describes these times:

> "After a heavy period of bicommunal meetings and training sessions between 1994 and 1997, all the meetings were banned and access was stopped in December 1997 by Turkish authorities. The excuse, the explanation, the justification for that decision was that the European Union at that year, at that month, decided not to discuss the possibility for giving Turkey a date to initiate negotiations for accession into the European Union. In reality, the actual reason behind it was the fact that everybody was overwhelmed by that citizen's movement and they feared that we were increasing in numbers, those crossing the line. In 1997, we had about 3,000 or 4,000 people who already had the opportunity to cross the line and meet people from the other side who wanted to continue, but they were not allowed to cross the line. So, that was a very good stimulation to find a solution to this problem. The Internet was a very good solution." [16]

---

13 Ibid.
14 Ibid.
15 Interview with Professor Diana Chinas on May 9, 2003.
16 Interview with Dr. Yiannis Laouris, Co-founder of Tech4Peace.org, June 2003.

Without any means to stay in touch, except three UN phone lines and occasional visits to Pyla, the bicommunal peace movement took on a new cyber dimension.

TECHNOLOGICAL PEACEBUILDING DEVELOPMENT HIGHLIGHTS

"Necessity is the mother of invention."
--Plato (428-348 B.C)

Cyprus was one of the last European countries to finally obtain Internet access not doing so until 1995. In the mid 1990s, several prescient Turkish and Greek Cypriots began to recognize the power of the Internet to enhance inter-communal communications.[17]

Several initiatives, some of which were self-funded or completely volunteer, started during this time. I will highlight the development of some of the more well-known technological initiatives. In the "Technological Roles and Applications" section of the book, we will examine some of these projects in further detail.

It is quite difficult to determine which initiative started first. In fact, the Internet in Cyprus was used as a mechanism to distribute negative propaganda before most of the online peace projects were established.

Technology for Peace (Tech4Peace.org)

During the summer of 1997, the Bicommunal Trainers Group's agora or bazaar brainstormed over 200 potential peace projects. Ultimately, 15 of the most timely and promising projects were selected. During the bazaar, these projects were presented to the larger number of people involved in bicommunal rapprochement, numbering over 200 at the time. A tech-

---

17   Interview with Dr. Yiannis Laouris, Co-founder of Tech4Peace.org, June 2003.

1

nology-based Internet project, called Technology for Peace, was included among these top 15 most important projects. [18]

Co-founder of Technology for Peace, Dr. Laouris, comments, "Cyprus was among the last countries on the planet to get access to the Internet."[19] This delay, according to Dr. Laouris, was due to both economic and political factors: "Many companies were controlled by the government; there was only one telecommunications company with a monopoly and they didn't want to introduce the Internet by allowing other companies to start Internet Service Providers. The government company delayed liberalization for many years. The other reason for the delay of the Internet to Cyprus was political in nature. The separation of the two communities in Cyprus is not only the fault of the Turkish side. The Greek side was also feeling very comfortable by keeping the people apart. The Internet would be a way to break the war in an individual way. There was no physical access or open telephone access at the time, so the Internet would be in contrast to that policy."[20]

During the initial stages of Internet adoption in 1996, Dr. Laouris worked with Dr. Hrach Gregorian in the United States through a USAID grant to set up some basic Internet infrastructure for intercommunal communications, called Technology for Peace. Dr. Laouris recollects the early days, "We had two teams on the island, one in the North and one in the South, and we set up kind of Internet cafes with a couple of computers at each side where peacebuilders could go and talk to people on the other side. This might sound today as very natural and very simplistic, but we are talking in a year where Internet was not even present. People didn't even know how to use the Internet. So, for Cyprus, it was very progressive. And, it gave the opportunity for people to stay in touch. In the framework of that project, we also did a mutual negotiation project."[21]

Dr. Gregorian expounds, "What we did back in the early 90s by today's standards, would be considered pretty primitive. The bottom line was that we were trying to capitalize on the availability of communication/technology at the time to try to overcome the most problematic challenge that we were facing with regard to regularized communication between Greek Cypriots

---

18   Cited per historical information of Tech4Peace.org website.
19   Interview with Dr. Yiannis Laouris, Co-founder of Tech4Peace.org, June 2003.
20   Ibid.
21   Interview with Dr. Yiannis Laouris, Co-founder of Tech4Peace.org, June 2003.

and Turkish Cypriots. So, what we did was, we established nodes either side of the green line with the understanding that initially, we would use this system that we had basically established there to do a little bit of work on what we used to call a VNEP, a Virtual Negotiation Project, through a simulation to ratchet up some of their basic skills in communication, negotiation, and other tools they would need to further their work. At the same time, to establish or to create capacity, particularly in the North, to communicate on a regular basis where there was a serious problem in terms of getting these people across the border, across the green line."[22]

Technology for Peace became the first officially funded Internet peace project in Cyprus with initial grants from USAID and USIP (United States Insititute of Peace). Once this funding expired, US-based Dr. Gregorian withdrew from the project, but the local Cypriot team continued their efforts and grant-seeking. With further funding, the Technology for Peace team set up a mailing service to put people on a list so that they could get the same message and distribute information very quickly. This network connected thousands of people. Eventually, with UN funding, the Technology for Peace initiative founded the Tech4Peace.org portal. According to Dr. Laouris, the concept of the portal was to create a flexible open space for many groups to publish and edit their own pages, announcements, etc. He contends, "It has played a major role in those years because it was the best communication tool we had. Since meetings were not allowed, it was our only way."[23] During this period, Tech4Peace.org grew into the largest peace portal in Cyprus and received funding from a variety of sources in addition to the United Nations.

Peace-Cyprus.org and Cyprus-Action.org

Another web portal, called Peace-Cyprus.org, played an instrumental role in online peacebuilding efforts. The organization behind the portal is very unique because it was founded by two Turkish Cypriots and two Greek Cypriots. Interestingly, the co-founders met on the Internet and carried out many initiatives together before ever meeting face-to-face. Eser Keskiner, co-founder of Peace-Cyprus.org reflects on their initial mission: "Although there were people involved in these activities (Track II Conflict Resolution

---

22 Interview with Dr. Hrach Gregorian, Director of World Affairs Institute, May 2003.
23 Interview with Dr. Yiannis Laouris, Co-founder of Tech4Peace.org, June 2003.

Workshops), it was not reaching the wide-scale population. Basically our goal, when we started, was to make sure that these events were no longer limited to a circle of elites, but anybody with an interest could go to our web pages and find announcements and also reports from the past events. So for a while, we were the only website doing such a thing."[24] It is important to note that Eser Keskiner participated in some of the early conflict resolution workshops.

Fellow Turkish co-founder, Turgut Durduran, a former Turkish Cypriot Fulbright scholar to the United States, comments on his earlier introduction to technology for peacebuilding in Cyprus:

> "I think I'm one of the first people to use it (Internet) for that purpose (peacebuilding). I came to the U.S. in 1993 as an undergrad student and when I came, there weren't even any web pages yet. What I found out about Cyprus, that there was a mailing list, which was a list which was set up in Turkey by a Turkish person. That list had Turkish and Greek Cypriots talking to each other. So that, I thought, was very interesting, so that I joined that list. In the meantime, I made some friends (over the Internet) that lived there, some Greek Cypriot friends. We began flirting with this idea. I think what we noticed was that it was a great idea to have Internet and at that time there were only, I think only, the Eastern Mediterranean University in North Cyprus had Internet access. No private access and only few providers in the South. So it mainly became a tool for top Cypriots, up road, to talk to each other. So we began advertising this list. We began advertising this list as a bi-communal forum for people to talk. In the meantime the web came about, so I set up a web page and then we got talking."

Durduran started a personal webpage at this time. This web page had some history, information about human rights, information about what was happening underground in Cyprus, including declarations of Turkish Cypriot and Greek Cypriot parties. Durduran continues:

---

24   Interview with Eser Keskiner Co-founder of Peace-Cyprus.org and Cyprus-Action.org, May 2003.

"In my sophomore year, which was, I think, the end of the year of 1994 in Maryland we had organized a workshop. Everybody who attended the workshop came from the mailing list and our announcement on the mailing list. That was sort of a good beginning. It was three days. I think only one day was devoted to the official training. The rest was more about what we picked up ourselves as discussions when we came together. By that time, people who were already involved in bi-communal work began using e-mail to talk to each other too, but it was still very limited. About 25 people attended our workshop this year. We got help from the Institute for Multi-Track Diplomacy (IMTD). During that time, I was getting more and more into it. At that time there was no Yahoo Group, no e-groups, so having mailing lists was really hard too. There was actually a Greek Cypriot mailing and the Turkish Cypriot mailing forum too. Through that, we got many people to join our activities. That is where I was mainly involved. Then the summer of 1995, we organized a big workshop for people who met through the Internet. At the end of that year we published a single issue of Bi-communal Journal too all on the Internet. I think it was about that time that Tech4Peace.org began receiving Government grants to start something with the previous technology."[25]

The founders of Peace-Cyprus.org also founded another organization called, Cyrpus-Action.org. Turgut Durduran explains, "Cyprus Action Network is more political, it's more for human rights, things like that. Peace Cyprus work is solely for public revolution and peacebuilding."[26]

Nicos' Email Newsletter
One of the most well known peacebuilders in Cyprus is Nicos Anastasiou. As a peace leader in Cyprus, he used technology as one of the most powerful tools to spread his messages, organize, and inform people all over the world.

---

25   Interview with Turgut Durduran, Co-founder of Peace-Cyprus.org and Cyprus-Action.org, May 2003.
26   Ibid.

Nicos is known for his email newsletter, which went out on a regular basis to over 7,000 people both in and outside of Cyprus, including politicians, diplomats, students, activists, and friends around the world.

Nicos started working with technology in the mid to late 90s. Nicos comments on his use of technology for peace: "This has evolved. It has not been designed. It has evolved spontaneously, naturally, as a response to the problems we face. As I often say when it comes to building the peace nothing can stop us. If plan a fails we go to plan b then we go to plan c. There is no grand plan. Things just happen in a natural 'one thing leads to another' kind of way. Part of it is initiative. Part of it is because something else has happened."[27]

Like many of the other virtual peacebuilders, Nicos participated in early conflict resolution training. He reflects on the influence of training:

"I wouldn't overemphasize the training that happened. I was involved in conflict resolution training workshops in 1994 and that's how I got into the process, but I would not say that that was the only parameter. I mean with the situation on the ground, there so many people and for me that was an opening that got me into this path, but in a way, I've been prepared all my life for this in that I grew up with Gandhi and Martin Luther King. When I came across these possibilities, something clicked and I said this is for me.... Everyone played a role and everyone played an important role, but I would not say that the role of foreign facilitators is the role; otherwise it would be a disaster kind a thing. Keep a reasonable balance there.... Right now that's a non-issue (conflict resolution training), it has no direct or indirect base in that it was a very useful and interesting starting point for me that happened in '94. After that everyday is volunteer work without getting paid. This is what I do. It's all volunteer, self-financed, and soul-driven! This is my house." [28]

(Nicos works from his home office.)

---

27   Interview with Nicos Anastasiou, January 2003.
28   Ibid.

Today Nicos actively engages in both online and off-line peacebuilding while working as a full-time schoolteacher. He is great source of motivation to many and is extraordinarily active in organizing events, demonstrations, and giving speeches.

CyprusMediaNet.com

Established in early 2003 and funded by the United Nations and the US State Department, CyprusMediaNet.com was a Cambridge Foundation for Peace project. This website allowed people, in Cyprus and around the world, to access accurate translations from the Greek Cypriot and Turkish Cypriot press in Greek, Turkish, and English. Dr. Prodromou, founder of the Cambridge Foundation for Peace, comments:

"Two-and-a-half years ago, I presented it (the project idea) to the U.S. Embassy in Cyprus and to USAID and at that time they didn't think the timing was auspicious. Given everything that's going on, or not going on, in terms of the efforts to make a political solution, this kind of a project that would really give the two community access to each other's media seems to me that the times right. They agreed and so that's how we revved things up and the proposal was accepted. The nice thing is that we've used all on-island talent for it, which is also, as you understand, part of the process. The aim of the project, obviously, was to give the two communities access to each other's media. Because what generally happens is that translations of media from either community are either from the most extreme articles or the most piece-knit, style articles. So the two communities weren't getting a representative sampling of what was being written in their respective presses about process of efforts to move toward and sustainable, political solution. So the idea was to bring a much more representative cross-section of translations of articles. They are word-for-word translations and they're real time of articles dealing with a range of categories—everything from economics to foreign policy to human interests. So again, to give them not only a representative cross-section in terms of, if you will, ideological or editorial approach to these issues, but also to give them a window into each other's community by talking about more than 'the Cyprus problem.' In some senses then, to use media and technology to humanize each other."[29]

Many off-island users, including members of the Greek and Turkish Cypriot Diasporas, Greeks and Turks abroad, and academics utilized this resource.

29   Interview with Dr. Elizabeth Prodromou, Founder of the Cambridge Foundation for Peace and CyprusMediaNet.com, Assoc. Dir., Inst. on Religion & World Affairs, Asst. Prof. Dept. of Int'l Relations Boston University, May 2003.

TECHNOLOGICAL ROLES AND APPLICATIONS

In attempting to understand the roles of technology in peacebuilding, along with practical applications, we should distinguish between a "conflict-centric" approach and reframing approach, which I refer to as "relational diplomacy." I consider conflict-centric approaches to focus on the issues and memory of the conflict, including much of the fear, pain, and resentment of the parties. I consider the "reframing approach" or relational diplomacy as a fresh way of looking at relationships among the parties. This concept deals with fostering interpersonal relationships, in the form of friendships, between the people on all levels. The focus of the "reframing" or relational diplomatic approach is to set the conflict aside completely and focus on the commonalities of the people, including similar personal interests across ingroup lines. The premise is that friendship is the first step to peace. Once parties understand and appreciate the humanity in the other, they can begin to focus on harder issues.

Dr. Apostilities of CyprusMediaNet.com refers to this way of thinking as a comparison of a glass half-full versus one half-empty. Shifting focus to positive friendships and cultural appreciation of the other is like looking at the glass half full. A conflict-centric approach is like looking at the glass half empty. [30] Dr. Anastasiou of Tech4Peace.org provides further insights:

> "There are two strands of approaches, both of which have been employed in Cyprus. On the one hand, we have had hundreds of workshops that actually attempted to address the conflicts. In

---

30   Interview with Dr. Dimitris Apostolidis, Program Coordinator for CyprusMediaNet.com, June 2003.

other words, to understand the perceptions of each community, to explicate the pain, to explicate the concerns, the fears, to envision how do we move forward, to envision possible peace-enhancing structures that have to come in and take the place of what is presently the situation. We have had think tanks that have worked on developing constitutional directives. We have had think tanks that have addressed the problem of education and the types of educational reform that were necessary to get away from reproducing the adversarial culture. So, you have this home multi-agnostic and strategic approach to the conflict, which really addresses the hard aspects of the conflicts and how to resolve them through non-violent means. Parallel to this at the same time, we have had another array of activity, which focused more on developing the culture of the future. Poets have gotten together. There is a bi-communal choir. There is a bi-communal dancing group. The choir and the group have actually done a number of events also in Turkey, which gained a lot of credibility and there was a lot of media coverage. It was the first experience for many people to actually see Greek and Turkish Cypriots dancing and singing together. So, these activities have more to do with building a culture of peace, a culture of tolerance, a culture of symbiosis, a culture which had enough space for the identity, the unique identity of each society, but also enough space and the kind of dynamic that could sustain a peaceful relationship between the two cultures. So, one strand of activities had more to do with trying to understand and address the hard aspects of the problem while as the other one has more to do with building those cultural and social elements which people envision to be part of the future society."[31]

I propose a more extensive definition:

Relational Diplomacy is an approach to sustainable peacebuilding, which recognizes that individual interpersonal relationships are the most essential and basic element—the building blocks for peace. The

---

31   Interview with Dr. Harry Anastasiou, Co-founder Tech4Peace.org, Professor of Conflict Resolution, Portland State University, May 2003.

relational diplomatic approach attempts to weave an intricate web of relationships among opposing parties to create bridges of understanding and friendship at various societal levels. Interconnectivity, based on mutual understanding, allows a fundamental shift in the perception of the other from fear to greater acceptance. Momentum towards sustainable peace expands exponentially as this relational constellation expands.

Technology can be used for both peacebuilding approaches, but the conflict-centric approach, based on talking through the issues of the conflict, best applies to professional conflict resolution training during the initial intervention statges. The reframing approach is perhaps more suitable for broader range citizen-based initiatives. In Cyprus, the conflict-centric approach was used earlier, in the mid 90s, and there has been a shift towards the reframing approach or relational diplomacy. Instead of debating the value of each, both seem to complement each other. As in the Cyprus problem, trainers can help build a peace constituency to carry out the reframing approach if the conflict-centric approach is used initially. Each conflict is unique, but certainly there are similarities. By understanding diverse world conflicts and a range of useful tools, peacebuilders will enhance their effectiveness in building sustainable peace.

BENEFITS OF TECHNOLOGY

My examination of the roles and applications of technology, with particular emphasis on implementation in Cyprus, addresses both the "conflict-centric" approach and the reframing approach. As Dr. Prodromou states, "I think that there's been, obviously, a strong success record for peacebuilders in Cyprus."[32] Let's explore some of the technological roles and applications. As we consider these applications, we must recognize an important caveat: In a sense, the potential of the Internet and technology is like a blank canvas. The final product is limited only by the skill and imagination of the practitioner. Here are some of the benefits created by peacebuilders in Cyprus and beyond who have used this technological canvas.

Enhances Educational Efforts

Track II actors have used technology for distance education. These programs include online courses in international negotiations, conflict resolution, and peace leadership. Some of these programs, such as the School of International Training's (SIT)'s Contact program in conflict resolution training, use a "place and space" concept in which participants spend most of the time online from diverse locations, but do come together once during the program to meet face-to-face. Dr. Ungerleider, director of SIT's Contact program, says this face-to-face encounter during the middle of the program "helps keep the energy going."[33] Many of the participants in the

---

32   Interview with Dr. Elizabeth Prodromou, Founder of the Cambridge Foundation for Peace and CyprusMediaNet.com, Assoc. Dir., Inst. on Religion & World Affairs, Asst. Prof. Dept. of Int'l Relations Boston University, May 2003.
33   Interview with Dr. John Ungerleider, Director of CONTACT program and Professor of Conflict Resolution at the School of International Training, Former US Fulbright Scholar to Cyprus, May 2003.

SIT program come directly from conflict areas, including Cyprus, Israel, Sri Lanka, etc. Online simulations, including negotiation games, also provide innovative new learning opportunities. Certainly, the distance education trend is rapidly increasing. Many reputable schools, such as The Fletcher School of Law and Diplomacy at Tuft's University and the Fuqua School of Business at Duke University offer distance education degree programs.

Creates Communication Bridges

As peacebuilders attempt to expand the interconnectedness of societies, the Internet facilitates bridge-building, and this was observed in Cyprus. Dr. Anastasiou recalls, "Unless you start building bridges across what we have called the Great Divide, you cannot really begin to address the conflict any creative way and, of course, meeting was very, very difficult. It was during this period when physical contact was impossible that cyberspace became meaningful because we would go through long periods of not being allowed to meet. What was very important for us is to sustain some sort of contact and some sort of communication."[34]

According to Dr. Gregorian, "I think for some communities it helped to prevent something like permanent estrangement, which was our biggest fear. If you keep people apart long enough, one or two generations, there's a real potential for permanent estrangement that's very dangerous. I think the technology helped to offset that. It was one of a number of tools. I can't say it was the principal reason, but it was not inconsequential in doing that and to other people, I think it provided a hope and they saw the possibilities even though the benefits may not have been immediately available to them. They saw the potential and that was a source of a great deal of hope and then finally, it provided a window to a larger world that would have been extremely difficult to provide through conventional media."[35]

Circumvents Traditional Barriers

The Internet provides a borderless venue for communications. Government efforts to limit access or Internet communications are quite difficult

---

34   Interview with Dr. Harry Anastasiou, Co-founder Tech4Peace.org, Professor of Conflict Resolution, Portland State University, May 2003.
35   Interview with Dr. Hrach Gregorian, Director of World Affairs Institute, May 2003.

to enforce. According to Dr. Anastasiou, "One of the assets (of technology) is that you cannot set up barbed wire and separate people in cyberspace so we thought that this is a very interesting kind of space, virtual space. If we couldn't meet physically, we would meet virtually."[36]

Dr. Gregorian comments about the initial introduction of technology in Cyprus, "The status-quo in Cyprus could be sustained as long as there was no contact. The regimes, especially the regime in the North, could not keep up with the technology; it could not realize what was going on. They thought just by hindering personal contact and phone calls, they would be able to prevent the contact of the people. But there was actually need from the people's side to reconcile the differences, to talk about things, to discuss what went wrong. People were finding every channel that they could find to overcome these issues and technology was definitely the easiest way, because the only other option was meeting in a third country, which not many people could do."[37]

Fosters Relationship Building

Peacebuilders in Cyprus have used the Internet as a way to incubate and build relationships among the sides. What proof do we have of the power of this invisible web between the Greek and Turkish Cypriots? Eser Keskiner of Peace-Cyprus.org provides some interesting evidence: "When the border was opened, most people were surprised that such a thing could happen. People were embracing each other, opening their homes, like having dinners together; it was if the division didn't exist. People looking from the surface may thing 'how did this happen,' I mean, all of the sudden. But it did not happen all of the sudden because discussions within both communities have been taking place for a long while."[38] Many of these relationships were developed during conflict resolution workshops and peace camps. Some of them were incubated through the Internet. Virtual communications certainly helped preserve many of these relationships.

---

36   Interview with Dr. Harry Anastasiou, Co-founder Tech4Peace.org, Professor of Conflict Resolution, Portland State University, May 2003.

37   Interview with Dr. Hrach Gregorian, Director of World Affairs Institute, May 2003.

38   Interview with Eser Keskiner Co-founder of Peace-Cyprus.org and Cyprus-Action.org, May 2003.

Nicos Anastasiou developed and administered an electronic matchmaking service during 1998-1999 when bicommunal meetings were banned completely. This service simply matched young people on either side of the green line electronically based on personal interests and hobbies. Nicos Anastasiou explains, "This girl likes music; here is another that likes music and dancing. We put them all together. We have the names of Greek Cypriots and these people have been matched with this Turkish Cypriots."[39] In the private sector, there is a proliferation of dating and friendship sites, which are quite successful using this model. Nicos was able to effectively apply this concept to peacebuilding. Most of Nicos' work was done through email and simple lists. A website database would have improved the administrative efficiency of this program. Even though the borders are now open, it is still difficult for people to make new friends, particularly with "the other." A matchmaking concept might even be more compelling now since people have the chance to meet in many areas beyond Pyla.

Fosters Relationship Preservation

The Fulbright Commission sponsored a peace camp run by the School of International Training (SIT) in Vermont. Seeds of Peace also conducted similar program for Greek and Turkish Cypriots to come together for team-building exercises and discussions with "the other." During these camps, friendships were formed among conflictants, but often these people returned to their home countries and lost touch. By building an online community, Seeds of Peace was able to help preserve and cultivate these friendships. Simple techniques, such as email and instantaneous chat, also helped encourage continued friendships.

Provides Safe Starting Point and Recruiting Grounds

People are often fearful of how their ingroup will view them if they associate with "the other." There is sometimes a fear of being labeled a traitor. The Internet provides a safe place to learn more and explore a new cause. Eser Keskiner of Peace-Cyprus.org explains, "When people get curious, they want to find out more about the other side. What do they do, they go on the Internet, they go to news groups and I have lots of friends from

---

39   Interview with Nicos Anastasiou, Peace Leader and Citizen Diplomat, January 2003.

the Internet. I actually studied in the U.S. I was lucky, I got to meet lots of Greek Cypriots. But I have friends who studied in Cyprus and even I would say from mid-'90's onwards, my friends in Cyprus would go on the Internet especially in search for people, Greek Cypriots, who they could talk to. Like on ICQ (Instantaneous chat), for example, they would look for people and I can tell you that these people, even before meeting each other, have lots of friends, that when the border's open, that's what you're seeing."[40]

Fosters Intercultural Understanding

The Internet provides a safe way to explore the identity of "the other" and also learn to appreciate "the other's" culture and traditions. There are a diverse range of options to provide intercultural awareness programs about "the other." Language is an important aspect of cultural understanding. Efforts on the Greek side to teach Greek online, i.e. programs on Kypros. net, were made available to Turkish Cypriots. The teaching of English was also viewed as an important way to provide a common neutral language in which conflictants might communicate. The Soros Foundation's Open Society Institute promotes the teaching of English as a common language to bridge conflicting societies in the South Caucasus.

Eser Keskiner explains, "I know some Turkish Cypriots who follow that course online (Greek language course). There was such a hunger for understanding the other people who would go on the Internet to learn the language of the other. That was a successful experiment."[41]

Provides Centralized Informational Source

Websites and email newsletters accumulate and distribute vast amounts of information. The Internet is increasingly becoming the predominant media outlet. Turgut Durduran explains, "There are a lot of newspapers that are now published on the net." As we have reviewed, CyprusMediaNet.com made articles available in English, Greek, and Turkish.[42]

---

40   Interview with Eser Keskiner Co-founder of Peace-Cyprus.org and Cyprus-Action.org, May 2003.
41   Interview with Eser Keskiner Co-founder of Peace-Cyprus.org and Cyprus-Action.org, May 2003.
42   Interview with Turgut Durduran, Co-founder of Peace-Cyprus.org and Cyprus-Action.org, May 2003.

Websites, such as Tech4Peace.org and Peace-Cyprus.org, and email newsletters listed a wide variety of information, including news, events and activities. As citizen-based efforts expand, the amount of peace-related activities can become daunting. Websites provide a centralized location for the distribution of information.

Nicos' newsletter tracked current events, including what he was immediately involved in and what other groups were doing. These newsletters often include links to photos and personal stories of participants. Nicos comments, "These messages are like a living journal. We do this because we don't have any other way to do the linking in terms of communications"[43]

There have been efforts in the past to publish a bicommunal magazine in Cyprus, called *Hade*. *Hade* is a word that both communities share in common and it means: "Let us go or let us move forward." *Hade* was made available in English, Greek, and Turkish. There were repeated attempts to gain UN Support to bring *Hade* back in the form of an online magazine. The USIA (US Information Agency), as part of its public diplomacy efforts, has used magazines as a way to promote the US image abroad. Such interactive bicommunal publications might also provide some mutual catharsis through the sharing of stories, poetry, music, art, photography, etc.

Enhances Accessibility and Reach

The goal of certain Track II programs is to reach certain influential members of the community who might have direct or indirect ties to policymakers. Track II initiatives often exclude a large population of potentially enthusiastic peacebuilders. Dr. Anastasiou describes the intention of Tech4Peace.org:

> "The inspiration behind that website which was also the rationale we gave to the United Nations in our application to secure the grant to set it up, was the idea that all these activities that were going on the ground were inaccessible to people. They were inaccessible for many reasons. First of all, the media within the island

---

43   Interview with Nicos Anastasiou, Peace Leader and Citizen diplomat, January 2003.

18

was not attendant because they were controversial. Because they were not in line with the traditional nationalist approach to the conflict. Because they were something quite new that didn't quite fit into the political culture of the island. And, because they were not adversarial basically. And, the media had absolutely no interest. So, the feeling we had was that all these events were taking place. There was a multiplication and an amplification of peacebuilding activities, which involved an increasing number of people. But, there was no record. So, our goal of Tech4Peace.org was to create a site that would be a kind of light inventory of all the peacebuilding activities. So, on the one hand, you have some sort of historical record, but more importantly, it became a reference point for other people who have questions—who wanted to find out more, who wanted to become involved, it became a reference point for people who could get a sense of what bi-communal contacts were all about, what peacebuilding was all about simply by surfing the web and visiting this particular website. And, indeed, it became that. It became that because checking the peace process through the Internet, as a first step, is a very safe way for people to explore whether they would like to get involved or not. But, it also became a reference point for politicians and for foreign diplomats. In fact, the American Embassy website in Cyprus also had a link to Tech-4Peace.org. So, it has multiple functions and the latest function is that it's a reference point for a number of who are interested in peacebuilding and who would like to explore test cases of citizen peacebuilding. So, the website has all these functions."[44]

Peace-Cyprus.org's Eser Keskiner comments, "The thing that Internet changed in Cyprus was basically to take the initiatives that were taking place within small groups and put it in the public domain. Both in terms of sharing the results and announcing these events." [45]

44   Interview with Dr. Harry Anastasiou, Co-founder Tech4Peace.org, Professor of Conflict Resolution, Portland State University, May 2003.
45   Interview with Eser Keskiner Co-founder of Peace-Cyprus.org and Cyprus-Action.org, May 2003.

Provides Vital Infrastructure and Continuity

Communications bridges lead to the establishment of vital infrastructure. Dr. Gregorian explains that in Cyprus, "These early tech projects were all designed to enhance communication and building more stable infrastructure for communication. The workshops everybody used to hold, including us, were often difficult to maintain the momentum and to keep people engaged and they tended, sometimes as they often do elsewhere, to be one-off deals. This was an attempt to build infrastructure in order to ensure some level of continuity because there was also the idea that we in the States would be part of the same network, and we could all work together."[46]

Facilitates Interdependent Bicommunal Projects

Bicommunal groups represent the core unit in the Cypriot peace initiative. These groups formed in a wide variety of ways—some through real world activities, i.e. peace camps and others completely online. Nicos Anastasiou sent his newsletter to over 30 bicommunal groups and took part in actively trying to form new groups. According to Nicos, one of the most successful groups was YAP 11, which focused on Cypriot dance. "There is a common Cypriot heritage," reiterates Nicos, "and they practice in Greek and Turkish."[47]

Nicos helped combine this dance group with another Cypriot music group and worked on arranging a tour of both sides of the island. This planning occurred primarily over the Internet.

Peace-Cyprus.org provided a tremendous example of bicommunal cooperation and teamwork. The founding members, two Greek Cypriots and two Turkish Cypriots, began working together on this project without ever meeting face to face. These former Fulbright Scholars worked together entirely on a volunteer basis.

Dr. Gregorian comments, "I can't think of a more powerful tool for consolidating people within communities and across communities at the grassroots level. There has never been a technology that could match the

---

46   Interview with Dr. Hrach Gregorian, Director of World Affairs Institute, May 2003.
47   Interview with Nicos Anastasiou, Peace Leader and Citizen Diplomat, January 2003.

capacity of digital or electronic-based communications in achieving this on a global scale, even on a national scale."[48]

Provides Organizational Tool

Peace leaders in Cyprus used the Internet to recruit and organize. Nicos Anastasiou explains "My position has more or less evolved into being a person who can send messages and coordinate things and using the technology that we have available do quite complicated projects and facilitate events that otherwise would be very difficult because it is so difficult and frustrating to meet face to face to plan things" [49]

Dr. Laouris, co-founder of Tech4Peace.org, considers the organizational strengths of technology:

"Technology forces you to get organized. For example, if there is a group of 10 who do peacebuilding and they need to communicate, they are looking for the telephone number or the address all the time to remember where I put this piece of card and pieces of paper and so forth. Technology means that if you want to send them an e-mail, you have to make a list. You have to have them all there. So, you push the button and there it goes. Second, it has everything there. You never lose it again. And, it's very quick to send e-mail to 10 people, but to give them a telephone call, you need one day to talk with them. What if you need to reach 1,000 people? So, this is one very important lesson. Another important lesson is that when you are using technology, there is no need for continued direct communication provided that you know the people."[50]

Provides Promotional Tool

Technology enhances the power to persuade and influence public opinion, and this was true in Cyprus. Dr. Gregorian refers to precursor technologies to the Internet: "The revolution in Iran was the 'cassette tape revolution.' What happened was Khomeini and other clerics' speeches and sermons were taped and those tapes were smuggled across the border and

---

48   Interview with Dr. Hrach Gregorian, Director of World Affairs Institute, May 2003.
49   Interview with Nicos Anastasiou, Peace Leader and Citizen Diplomat, January 2003.
50   Interview with Dr. Yiannis Laouris, Co-founder of Tech4Peace.org, June 2003.

they basically were the source of most of the information that the people who eventually supported the revolution relied on. Whether the change was for the good or not is another matter entirely, but you can see where the technology played a very important role."[51]

Of course, forces of evil are just as capable of harnessing the power of technology to influence opinion and recruit members. Al Qaeda is very adept at organizing and recruiting members, as well as promoting its message, via the Internet.

Dr. Anastasiou indicates the negative governmental intentions related to Internet usage:

"When the Internet was introduced in Cyprus, one of the main motives for actually introducing it and changing the legislation to make it happen was the concern by some hard liners that one side was conducting propaganda through the Internet and therefore, the other side has to do the same. Indeed, the conflict has been taken into cyberspace. The difficulty that we had in the past is that the other (hate) websites were there but there was no alternative. Now we have employed technology to represent an alternative approach, an alternative voice to dealing with the problems. So, there is this kind of rivalry on the net and you find it in every conflict. You know, it's nothing new. But, in a sense, what we have attempted to do is to explore peace-enhancing uses of the same technology." [52]

The online peace initiatives have been able to erode the effects of online negative propaganda in Cyprus. Fortunately, the momentum has shifted towards peace. Dr. Anastasiou describes this phenomenon, "Most of the work that was done, especially by citizens, had this very subtle impact on the rest of the system. It sort of operated right beneath the surface and it did help erode the traditional nationalism that the society inherited. It's really a long process." [53]

51   Interview with Dr. Hrach Gregorian, Director of World Affairs Institute, May 2003.
52   Interview with Dr. Harry Anastasiou, Co-founder Tech4Peace.org, Professor of Conflict Resolution, Portland State University, May 2003.
53   Ibid.

Connects Populations in Diaspora

In any discussion of technological peacebuilding, diaspora populations should be considered. Diaspora communities often have more severe, less compromising views of "the other."[54]

The traditional role of the nation-state is being challenged as theorists make a call for a social science that is "unbound" from the nation-state, one that recognizes the existence of "transnational social field" or "transnational social spaces."[55] Professor Thomas Faist describes these social spaces as:

> "Transnational communities characterize situations in which international movers and dense and strong social and symbolic ties connect stayers over time and across space to patterns of networks and circuits in two countries. Such communities without propinquity do not necessarily require individual persons living in two worlds simultaneously or between cultures in a total "global village" deterritorialized space. What is required, however, is that communities without propinquity link through exchange, reciprocity, and solidarity to achieve a high degree of social cohesion and a common repertoire of symbolic and collective representations."[56]

Through intricate transnational interconnectedness, diaspora populations influence local efforts and worldwide opinion. These groups must also participate in the peacebuilding activities. Given the global sporadic disbursement of these groups, the Internet provides one of the only viable alternatives for creating bridges among these populations.

---

54 Interview with Dr. Elizabeth Prodromou, Founder of the Cambridge Foundation for Peace and CyprusMediaNet.com, Assoc. Dir., Inst. on Religion & World Affairs, Asst. Prof. Dept. of Int'l Relations Boston University, May 2003.
55 Peter Kivisto, *21st Century Sociology: Multiculturalism in a Global Society*, Blackwell Publishing, Oxford, 2002, p. 38.
56 Ibid.

ADDITIONAL USEFUL TECHNOLOGIES

IRC (Instantaneous Chat)

Peace-Cyprus.org used communal IRC, a chat room, to bring people together. Turgut Durduran claims that this is more personal than email. Currently, ICQ technology offers the ability to have private chats online as well. Additionally, there are some free Internet telephone services that offer interesting options for parties to talk with "the other."

Listservs (E-Groups) and Email Messaging

Nicos Anastasiou sent peacebuilding messages to over 7,000 people on both sides of the conflict with the click of one button. Many of these 7,000 people forwarded their messages to others. Recipients included academics, practitioners, NGOs, government officials, foreign diplomats, students, and many other people interested in the Cyprus problem all over the world. Nicos' newsletters were the most common way many people kept in touch with the Cyprus problem. In addition to inspirational messages, Nicos's mass mailer included: information about events, activities, and progress; encouragement for people to get involved; and messages or news directly from other parties. These mailers were very effective because of their proactive nature. They reached out and grabbed the recipients without requiring recipients to visit a website.

According to Eser Keskiner, "The Internet, and more specifically e-mail, totally changed things because people were able to form mail groups and start discussing issues. So suddenly the issue was not at the monopoly of the political leaderships who would go and meet each other and go out and say something to their own people, but not necessary reflect what actually took place there. So, technology has opened the channel for people to actually start discussing on their own. There are mail groups about general discussion about Cyprus that have been active for almost ten years now. They're extremely successful; they have built their own communities. I know, for example, there is a mailing group which is basically a big community. They hold meetings in Cyprus, they hold meetings in London, so people moved from the virtual community to the real communities."[57] Online communities provide opportunities instilling a sense of cooperation and connection beyond traditional ingroup associations. The private sector provides many examples of supranational online communities; peacebuilders have much to learn from the for-profit world in this area.

Turgut Durduran adds, "E-mail was basically the only way we could communicate at that time. Only within the last month, the telephone lines have begun working between two sides and now cross-visits were allowed but that was really effective."[58]

In January 2003, close to 70,000 Cypriots amassed in Nicosia to demonstrate for peace. These demonstrations were organized primarily through email message to computers and mobile phones.

Online Bulletin (Threaded Discussion) Boards

Tech4Peace.org and Peace-Cyprus.org had discussion boards for both interactive dialogue and organizational efforts. Arthur Martirosyan, Director of the Momentum Project, suggests a moderator and agreement to guidelines for exchange online. Certain personal guarantees to conduct will help ensure respectful communications.[59]

Audio/Video Presentations

Presentation options are limited only by peacebuilders' imaginations. There are plentiful software options to record video, audio, or slide presentations. These programs might be used for both Track II and citizen diplomacy efforts. There is currently an initiative underway in Cyprus to present personal stories of Greek and Turkish Cypriots online through video clips

---

57   Interview with Eser Keskiner Co-founder of Peace-Cyprus.org and Cyprus-Action.org, May 2003.
58   Interview with Turgut Durduran, Co-founder of Peace-Cyprus.org and Cyprus-Action.org, May 2003.
59   Interview with Arthur Martirosyan, Director of the Momentum Project, Conflict Management Group, May 2003.

Radio Shows

Radio shows are an important way to influence wide audiences. The Voice of America has been an effective way for the US government to promote its image abroad. In Africa, radio is an essential means of reaching audiences with positive and negative messages, i.e. Rwanda. Web-based radio is also a growing area.

TV Programming/Live Streaming Webcasts

Peacebuilders sometimes use TV as a forum for reaching wide audiences. Dr. Gregorian cites some particularly effective work in this medium: "A Search for Common Ground did these great video projects in Macedonia on tolerance and cross-ethnic cross-cultural communication. They were like Sesame Street-type of programs. They also have done a good deal of radio programming and radio drama that is broadcast in Africa where most people get most of their information orally and from, as far as technology go, radios rather than televisions and newspapers and such."[60] With technological advancement, we will most likely experience more media convergence and an increasing popularity for web TV.

Streaming webcasts offer interesting possibilities for peacebuilders as well. This technology allows live feeds into events, i.e. lectures, seminars, demonstrations, cultural events, etc. Such technology might prove particularly useful to diaspora populations striving to keep up-to-date on activities.

Audio Chat/Video Chat (Teleconferencing)

Both Peace-Cyprus.org and Tech4Peace.org explored options for audio and video chat, including teleconferencing and web conferencing. Audio and video chats enhance the sensual encounter with "the other." This technology is currently used more and more by online private sector entertainment communities and for business interactions. There are relatively inexpensive software packages for audio/video chat. There is also the opportunity to use audio and video chats for online interactive lessons, i.e. teaching about "the other." Englishtown.com teaches English entirely online to over 3,000,000 worldwide members using this type of technology.

---

60   Interview with Dr. Hrach Gregorian, Director of World Affairs Institute, May 2003.

OBSTACLES

The Internet and other tech-based initiatives do not provide the panacea to peacebuilding; instead new technologies should be viewed as tools to empower and expand peacebuilders' interventional choices. In order to design responsible and effective online interventions, inherent risks and limitations to virtual peacebuilding must be considered. We can learn from some of the primary challenges faced by tech-based peacebuilders in Cyprus.

Language Barriers

Language differences present both difficulties and advantages for communications among conflictants. In Cyprus, Dr. Anastasiou explains, "The first language that was used for peacebuilding was English. It sort of happened by default because most Greeks cannot speak Turkish. More Turks speak Greek, but now, you have a new generation that has no contact with Greece. Increasingly, the level of education has risen and more people in the mainstream middle class in Cyprus can communicate fairly well in the English language. English became a kind of mediatory language, if you will. In a very subtle way, it solved the problem of deciding which language we were going to use. So, it came in a sense as an aide."[61] In this sense, English provided a neutral language for communications. As indicated earlier, many organizations, such as the Soros Foundation's Open Society Institute, are supporting English language education as a method to enhance democratization and sustainable peace.

Language barriers present greater obstacles in areas without an English-speaking constituency. Eser Keskiner comments, "English serves, most of

---

61   Interview with Dr. Harry Anastasiou, Co-founder Tech4peace.org, Professor of Conflict Resolution, Portland State University, May 2003.

the time, as the language of peacebuilders, which limits the scope. Hopefully, there will be chances for people to communicate in their own language. For that, there will be need for teaching of Turkish and Greek to respective communities and where not possible, the peacebuilding events ideally would have simultaneous translators. Which I'm aware is a very difficult process, but in order to open the process up further to the rest of the people, it's a necessary step." [62]

In Cyprus, English communications still present problems. According to Dr. Laouris, "People are not as fluent in writing as they are in speaking. When they speak, they can speak for 10 minutes and share their ideas. But, when they write, they don't have the same courage to write for 10 minutes, so they write shortly. It's also good because you are forced to be concise and brief. But, at the same time, it's bad because it cannot expand and brainstorm."[63]

Many Cypriot peacebuilders have reacted positively to using English since their language skills have increased.

Evaluations/Lack of Research of Technological Applications

Many of the difficulties of evaluating technological initiatives are encountered by traditional peacebuilders as well. There is great difficulty in tracing the cause and effect of events back to one particular intervention. Author and peacebuilder John Lederach distinguishes between content goals and relational goals: "Content goals relate to what people want and need in terms of the substance of the conflict. These are often the visible issues we debate, argue, and fight over. Relational goals are those goals that correspond to the questions of who we are to one another: the influence, the distance or proximity, and the level of interdependence that we seek and/ or grant one another. Peacebuilding is concerned both with finding ways to deal with the issues in a conflict and with redefining the relationship."[64]

62   Interview with Eser Keskiner Co-founder of Peace-Cyprus.org and Cyprus-Action.org, May 2003.
63   Interview with Dr. Yiannis Laouris, Co-founder of Tech4Peace.org, June 2003.
64   John Paul Lederach, *Building Peace: Sustainable Reconciliation in Divided Societies*, Washington, D.C.: United States Institute of Peace Press, 1997, p. 134.

Content goals certainly are more easily analyzed than improvements in societal relationships. Lederach points to the importance of talking about sustaining process-structure, not just about sustaining outcome.[65] The "theory-based" approach of Carol Weiss might offer an interesting evaluatory option. Weiss' work suggests that rather than working with standard evaluation methods, community initiatives should be based on the "theories of change" that underlie the work conducted.[66]

There is no generic format to measure tech-based technological initiatives and views about evaluations vary. Dr. Dimitris Apostolidis of CyprusMediaNet.com must measure results of the online translation project through tracking web traffic and readership diversity. Funders demand continual statistics on progress and market penetration.[67]

On the other hand, Dr. Anastasiou of the web-based Tech4Peace.org portal, comments: "You cannot approach technology outside of how it's conceptualized and how it's integrated into the community's concern. I wouldn't be able to get a handle on it, actually to do an evaluation of technology-based programs because in a sense there are no technology-based programs, at least that we have used. We have had programs that had to do with people, that had to do with a specific agenda, that had to do with popularizing a new approach to the conflicts, and within that context, technology gave us a certain facility. So, the role of technology for us has been meaningful only as a subsidiary component of the human and cultural dimensions that were at stake."[68]

Technologies are so new and experimental that many practitioners are not sure about how to evaluate outcomes. Dr. Prodromou refers to the National Endowment for Democracy which does a lot with technology and democratization work and mentions that it is quite difficult to get a sense of how they evaluate the returns on the ways that they use technology.[69]

---

65   Ibid.
66   Ibid.
67   Interview with Dr. Dimitris Apostolidis, Program Coordinator for CyprusMediaNet.com, June 2003.
68   Interview with Dr. Harry Anastasiou, Co-founder Tech4peace.org, Professor of Conflict Resolution, Portland State University, May 2003.
69   Interview with Dr. Elizabeth Prodromou, Founder of the Cambridge Foundation for Peace and CyprusMediaNet.com, Assoc. Dir., Inst. on Religion & World Affairs, Asst. Prof. Dept. of Int'l Relations Boston University, May 2003.

Regarding the use of technology for peacebuilding, Boston University's Dr. Prodromou comments, "I don't really think there's any good research out there"[70] Given the inherent difficulties in evaluating peacebuilding in general, the results of tech-based initiatives, unless restricted to numerical user rates, will perhaps remain even more illusive.

Sustainability

The first virtual negotiations project started by Dr. Gregorian, Dr. Laouris, and others received short-lived funding for 1.5 years. Dr. Gregorian recalls, "We ran out of money before we ran out of ideas."[71] Fortunately, Dr. Laouris and his partners continued on with Tech4Peace.org, which has now turned into an important peace portal in Cyprus, funded by the United Nations among others. It should be noted that many peacebuilding efforts, including Nicos's newsletter, reaching over 7,000 people, and Peace-Cyprus.org survived solely through volunteer support. In fact, financial donations have been refused to avoid funder control and preserve both impartiality and bicommunal public trust. Cyprus-Peace.org's Eser Keskiner comments, "We don't get funding. Everything that we do comes out of our own pockets. It's totally volunteer-based and in a way that was how we wanted it to be. Because once you get into the funding trouble, there will be people from both sides trying to label you as serving the interests of x, or y, or z, depending on who the funds are coming from. So we try to stay neutral, but how that may change in the future, I don't know."[72]

Impartiality and Objectivity

Large payments for peace projects sometimes raise questions, especially about impartiality and objectivity. Dr. Prodromou comments:

> "I think that the so-called Track II industry have made a lot of money out of Cyprus. I'm quite cynical, quite candidly, when it comes to them. I think that the issue of impartiality and objectivity is always a challenge for any organization. I think in some ways

70   Ibid.
71   Interview with Dr. Hrach Gregorian, Director of World Affairs Institute, May 2003.
72   Interview with Eser Keskiner Co-founder of Peace-Cyprus.org and Cyprus-Action.org, May 2003.

the peacebuilding or Track II practitioners have become a voice in the Cyprus and I think that's been to the detriment of a solution. Recognizing the heterogeneity of the Turkish Cypriot community, I don't think that Track II'ers did a good job, particularly in so far as they had regular access to the Turkish Cypriot community in giving a nuanced picture of how variegated that community was. I can offer a very specific example. The long-standing view of the Turkish Cypriot community was that it was monolith, that everyone supported Denktas, that fears about security based on past experiences were so great that there really wasn't any alternative Turkish Cypriot voice. That's certainly never a view I held to. Now, in the last year, that's clearly a view that has not only been discredited, but it's one that has been critiqued regularly and publicly by policy builders. That's a view that, in my experience, was one perpetuated by Track II participants. I think Cyprus shows an over capacity when it comes to Track II peacebuilding. Organizations oftentimes make those very actors part of the problem or part of the process, at least, in a way that I would suggest should be avoided. I think that Track II is intended to give voice to the actors and participants in the problem, not to become a voice in the problem." [73]

The area of financial rewards is wrought with internal rivalries among practitioners and citizen diplomats. Limited fund availability unfortunately necessitates competition among peacebuilders. This remains an obstacle to cooperation.

Collaboration and Cooperation

How does a proliferation of peacebuilders, both Track II and citizen-based, influence the environment? In development work, a proliferation of actors might actually harm an environment. As author Mary Anderson suggests, "introducing resources into a resource-scarce environment where there is conflict usually increases competition and suspicion among

---

73   Interview with Dr. Elizabeth Prodromou, Founder of the Cambridge Foundation for Peace and CyprusMediaNet.com, Assoc. Dir., Inst. on Religion & World Affairs, Asst. Prof. Dept. of Int'l Relations Boston University, May 2003.

warring parties."[74] This assertion does not necessarily apply to conflict resolution interventions. In fact, the objective of many intervention programs, such as the Track II "training of trainers," is to encourage a diverse group of participants to build and spread their own programs within the society. The peacebuilding *agora* or bazaar in 1997 in Cyprus illustrates this intent. Similarly, technology-based initiatives, while often competing, do reach diverse populations and help build positive momentum.

Contrary to development work, actor proliferation in peacebuilding is viewed positively; however, greater coordination is required and local voices must be empowered. Pamela Aall of the Institute of Peace reports, "With so many actors at different levels of the international system available to intervene in complex emergencies, coordination is essential to avoid overlapping and counterproductive responses that result in wasted resources and inefficient operations. In a crisis situation, so many different things occur simultaneously that one actor often does not know what the others are doing. People operating at the grass-roots level are often considered unimportant or peripheral by those operating at higher levels. A successful intervention, nonetheless, call for the ability to understand and connect the different levels of activity."[75]

NGOs and citizens groups often have difficulty in working together. In Cyprus, two of the largest peace portals, Tech4Peace.org and Peace-Cyprus.org, work on parallel tracks towards similar goals. Tech4Peace.org has received significant funding from the United Nations, whereas Peace-Cyprus.org has shied away from funding to maintain impartiality. Turgut Durduran, co-founder of Peace-Cyprus.org comments about associations with Tech4Peace.org: "We did have some amount of collaboration with Tech4Peace.org at some point. But then they were some issues related to it, let's put it that way."[76] Eser Keskiner, another co-founder of Peace-Cyprus. org remarks, "Basically in times of need, in times when there is common

---

74   Mary B. Anderson, *Do No Harm: Supporting Local Capacities for Peace through Aid*. Cambridge, Mass.: Local Capacities for Peace Project/ Collaborative for Development Action, Inc., 1996.

75   Chester A. Crocker, Fen Osler Hampson with Pamela Aall, *Managing Global Conflict: Sources of and Responses to International Conflict*, United States Institute of Peace Press: Washington, D.C. 1996, p. 440.

76   Interview with Turgut Durduran, Co-founder of Peace-Cyprus.org and Cyprus-Action.org, May 2003.

action needed, these groups do come together. But each group, at the same time, maintains its own identity." [77]

In addition to funding disparities, ideological approaches also inhibit cooperation. Some of the peacebuilder portals, such as Cyprus Action Network (Cyprus-Action.org) are focusing on human rights activism, while other sites attempt to remain neutral or apolitical.

One of the goals of the Tech4Peace.org website is to act as a compendium of activities. Nicos's newsletters also act as an information source. Ultimately, informational sources also compete for users and funds.

Capacity

The use of technology presupposes a certain technological and economic infrastructure. The use of technology is limited by availability and prevalence of users. In some regions, other more simplistic technological tools are useful. In Africa, peacebuilders rely heavily on radio programming. As Dr. Gregorian mentioned, the revolution in Iran is often called the 'cassette tape revolution' because Ayatollah Khomeini's speeches were distributed on tape. People use whatever means are available to spread their message. [78]

Turgut Durduran comments, "The biggest problem was accessibility. Only in the last few years, people are having Internet in their own home and the providers are everywhere. So before then, people underground in Cyprus, especially older people, activist, politicians and such people were not that keen on using Internet. They still preferred to try to make a phone call through the United Nations line, or try to get their pieces and articles across the border through some UN diplomat or something."[79]

During the early stages of technology use, the infrastructure was more developed in the South of Cyprus. Still today, the South is economically and technologically more advanced. Dr. Gregorian recalls about the slow speed of the early virtual negotiation project, "The South just didn't have the patience, and I didn't blame them to stay on with the slow pace of messages and other communication back and forth." [80]

---

77   Interview with Eser Keskiner Co-founder of Peace-Cyprus.org and Cyprus-Action.org, May 2003.

78   Interview with Dr. Hrach Gregorian, Director of World Affairs Institute, May 2003.

79   Interview with Turgut Durduran, Co-founder of Peace-Cyprus.org and Cyprus-Action.org, May 2003.

80   Interivew with Dr. Hrach Gregorian, Director of World Affairs Institute, May 2003.

Internet uses are also quite expensive in some areas of the world. Many are unable to afford heavy usage. People must have the economic means to participate; this leads to further segmentation. Eser Keskiner remarks: "The initial goal of his peace portal was to get the processes out of the group of elites and open it up to the public sphere, which is not entirely possible because not everyone has access. Unfortunately, this has been a shortcoming that we had to live with." [81]

Technological Adaptation Issues

Reactions to the Internet are often regarded with cautious enthusiasm. Using new technologies can also be quite intimidating. The learning curve is often steep and there are barriers to entry for users. As technological usage proliferates around the world, people will become more comfortable with using technology. This often takes time. As Eser Keskiner of Peace-Cyprus.org explains, "The advantage with Cyprus is it's a small community. So there is the domino effect of one person knowing. That means that ten people around that person are going to start getting involved and questioning things too."

Peacebuilders must consider who they are trying to reach to determine which tools, i.e. technological peacebuilding, will work most effectively.

Transparency and Legitimacy

Peacebuilding activities often conjure up suspicion about ingroup loyalties. Combine a technological aspect to these efforts and questions about an operation's integrity expand exponentially.

Dr. Prodromou comments, "One of my concerns, frankly, about technology and peacebuilding is the credibility of the legitimacy of whatever projects that might be out there. Particularly one when you get into using the Internet and that's more of an Internet problem than it is technology in peacebuilding."[82]

---

81   Interview with Eser Keskiner Co-founder of Peace-Cyprus.org and Cyprus-Action.org, May 2003.

82   Interview with Dr. Elizabeth Prodromou, Founder of the Cambridge Foundation for Peace and CyprusMediaNet.com, Assoc. Dir., Inst. on Religion & World Affairs, Asst. Prof. Dept. of Int'l Relations Boston University, May 2003.

Issues of legitimacy and transparency are not confined to virtual domains. Authors Prendergrast and Plumb point out, "Civil Society Organizations (CSOs) are not by definition virtuous; they can be political, corrupt, and as prone to exacerbating conflict as they are to resolving it."[83] The appearance of a website alone can provide a certain amount of legitimacy. In many cases, it is difficult to ascertain the size, leadership, or potential ulterior motives of a technology-based enterprise; however, a technological presence, if used responsibly, can allow a greater degree of transparency. Many organizations even post financial records on the web.

Professor Eileen Babbitt cites the guiding principle of many crisis resolution practitioners as "do no harm" and indicates, in the case of trainers, "At a minimum, trainers should leave a situation no worse off than when they arrived." [84]

Ultimately, given the proliferation of professional Track II and citizen actors, higher standards should be set to assure transparency and legitimacy. At the very minimum, participants must beware.

Content/Project Quality

The Internet is a medium—a new resource for peacebuilders. It is up to peacebuilders to provide creative, innovative, and appropriate interventions. As Dr. Gregorian suggests, "The technology is just breathtaking in terms of the numbers of people it can reach across the expanse. But, it's still the case unless you have substance, the technology—no matter how jazzy and how attractive it is visually and such cannot carry you if you don't have the content, the substantive content that drives these things."[85] It is tremendously time-consuming work to build and update content for technological initiatives. In the private sector, full-time content managers often handle this daunting task. Dr. Anastasiou comments on the explosion of activities in Cyprus: "In some cases, the number of things (on the site) are

---

83   John Prendergrast and Emily Plumb , "Building Local Capacity: From Implementation to Peacebuilding", in Stephen Stedman, Donald Rotchild and Elizabeth Cousens, *Enging Civil Wars,* Lynne Rienner, 2002, p. 328.

84   Eileen Babbitt, "Contributions of Training to International Conflict Resolution" in William Zartman, J. Lewis Rasmussen, *Peacemaking in International Conflict: Methods and Techniques*, Washington, D.C.: United States Institute of Peace Press, 1997, p. 365.

85   Interview with Dr. Hrach Gregorian, Director of World Affairs Institute, May 2003.

either outdated or a number of other things seem to not be represented simply because it has become increasingly difficult to collect information and upload it. This is perhaps the greatest challenge to grasp the technology in some sort of institutionalized process that can collect the new information and post it."[86] Tech-based peacebuilders must also enlist professionals, i.e. conflict resolution specialists, to monitor or participate in online programs to ensure quality. This is sometimes a hard sell.

Government Intervention

Many of the early tech-based peacebuilders encountered governments threats. Dr. Gregorian praised their brave efforts, especially in the North of Cyprus, during these early times; these interventions caused a great deal of fear. Turkish Cypriot Turgut Durduran comments, "There were a lot of attacks against us. Our e-mails were taken to the police, they were taken to military, and we were harassed by the government and things like that as well."[87] A subsequent proliferation of users has made it difficult for government interference. Although not impenetrable, the Internet usually provides a safe environment for peace activities.

Assaults

The anonymity of the Internet, if not properly monitored, can allow for mean-spirited attacks among online participants in certain virtual forums, i.e. discussion boards. Dr. Gregorian cautions, "People can get on and trash other people and can disrupt systems and can use it for propagandist purposes. Further certain track one actors, that is to say regimes, can use it to identify folks that they may want to marginalize if not eliminate politically. There is nothing about the technology that necessarily pushes it in the direction of necessarily more peaceful activity. It's still a matter of folks who, with good intentions, and with the proper sort of philosophical bent to pushing it rather than the technology pushing the people."[88] Moderators, guidelines, and restrictions on usage, such as password/member

---

86   Interview with Dr. Harry Anastasiou, Co-founder Tech4peace.org, Professor of Conflict Resolution, Portland State University, May 2003.
87   Interview with Turgut Durduran, Co-founder of Peace-Cyprus.org and Cyprus-Action.org, May 2003.
88   Interview with Dr. Hrach Gregorian, Director of World Affairs Institute, May 2003.

removal, mitigate some of these risks. Virtual programs must factor in these potentialities.

Misunderstandings

According to Dr. Laouris, "The major obstacle is misunderstandings. You don't have the human contact, the smile that might accompany a bad word that you might use, especially when you use another language, you might not use the right word and it can be understood in a different way. Even if you speak with somebody, if it is misunderstood, a smile will wash away the possible misunderstanding. But, in written language, you don't have a second chance to fix it. If you write something that disturbs somebody, it's there and it harms the relationship."[89]

Issues of Senior Level Project Control

In some cases, particularly in less technologically friendly environments, senior staff is threatened by more technologically savvy junior people taking over control. Dr. Gregorian points out, "It's the junior members of the staff that have the tech savvy and the linguistic skills and a sufficient level of sophistication in the whole conceptual realm that they run rings around these guys (senior members). What happens is that the senior people feel threatened and pretty soon, the junior people can no longer operate as effectively if at all as they did while we were there."[90] Generational changes will slowly allow for greater technological integration across all levels.

---

89   Interview with Dr. Yiannis Laouris, Co-founder of Tech4Peace.org, June 2003.
90   Interview with Dr. Hrach Gregorian, Director of World Affairs Institute, May 2003.

THEORETICAL CONSIDERATIONS

We have examined many of the practical applications and limitations of technology in peacebuilding with a particular focus on the Cyprus conflict. Are these technological interventions rooted in conflict resolution theory? Can such theory take the technological leap? At this stage it is important to compare and contrast theory with technologically based practice. In addition to delving into conflict resolution theory, we will also explore elements of intercultural communications theory, social psychology, and public diplomacy.

Conflict Resolution Theory
Protracted Social Conflict

According to educator Edward Azar, a new type of conflict called protracted social conflict (PSC), has increased in prevalence since World War II[91]. PSC occurs among diverse religious, racial, or cultural communal groups and originates as these groups strive to maintain and protect their distinctive identities.[92] Azar points to over 60 examples of protracted social conflict around the world, including Cyprus, Israel, Sri Lanka, South Africa, etc.[93] Most of these protracted social conflicts are intranational in scope and more akin to communal or intercommunal conflict than international conflict.[94]

Since protracted social conflict is rooted deeply in the societal need to protect and maintain distinctive group identity, traditional diplomacy is

---

91   Edward Azar, "The analysis and Management of Protracted Conflict," in *The Psychodynamics of International Relationships* (vol. 2) by V. Volkan, J. Montvlle and D. Julius (1991). p.1.

92   Ibid p.3.

93   Ibid, p.1.

94   John Paul Lederach, *Building Peace: Sustainable Reconciliation in Divided Societies*, Washington, D.C.: United States Institute of Peace Press, 1997, p12.

unlikely to yield sustainable peace. These conflicts are embedded into the hearts and minds of the people. Traditional diplomacy is more equipped to resolve resource-based issues (e.g., control over land, poverty, power-sharing, distribution of economic opportunities).[95]

The deeper human needs and values, involving issues of identity, survival, and fears, must be addressed by changing the underlying human relationship, promoting mutual understanding and acknowledgement of these concerns.[96]

This is where the need for citizen diplomacy enters the stage. Technology bridges the human divide and allows communication among a mass group of individuals, thus affecting the hearts and minds of the people.

Stereotypes and Images

According to author Elizabeth Bronfen, "The stereotype of 'the other' is used to control the ambivalent and to create boundaries. Stereotypes are a way of dealing with the instabilities arising from the division between self and non-self by preserving an illusion of control and order.[97] Stereotypical myths of 'the other' protect existing structures and relations of power behind the shield of 'safe legitimacy.'"[98]

John Lederach suggests that protracted social conflicts have roots in long-standing distrust, fear, and paranoia, which are reinforced by the immediate experience of violence, division, and atrocities. This experience further exacerbates the hatred and fear that are fueling the conflict.[99] In divided societies, conflictants often have radically differing perceptions of each other.[100] The fears of these subgroups are manipulated by leaders to retain control.[101]

---

95   Diana Chigas, *Negotiating Intractable Conflicts: The Contributions of Unofficial Intermediaries*, Draft in process of United States Institute of Peace, 2003.
96   Ibid.
97   Elisabeth Bronfen, 1992: 182, in Michael Pickering, *Stereotyping: The Politics of Representation*, New York: Palgrave Press, 2001, p. 47.
98   Ibid., p. 48.
99   John Paul Lederach, *Building Peace: Sustainable Reconciliation in Divided Societies*, Washington, D.C.: United States Institute of Peace Press, 1997, p. 13.
100   Ibid.
101   Ibid.

According to social psychologists, humans bolster their self-identity by identifying with a group. Group associations are usually mutually exclusive and involve the creation of an ingroup and an outgroup. This labeling responds to deep social-psychological needs, can lead to the creation of enemy stereotypes, and can culminate in conflict.[102]

In divided societies, such as Cyprus, separate structures organized on the basis of identity prevent the cross-pollination of ideas and exchange. In this kind of society, creating and maintaining ethnic stereotypes and enemy images is easy.[103] A cycle of reciprocal behavior then reinforces adversary images by providing allegedly confirming evidence of hostile intentions. Enemy images tend to become self-fulfilling and self-reinforcing."[104]

Without interventions at every opportunity to dislodge this perpetual reaffirming effect, this unfortunate and intractable cycle will persist. Technology provides diverse and creative mechanisms for psychological interventions.

Focusing on the substantive issues only addresses a very small part of the problem. Cultural understanding must be fostered prior to, during, and after resolution of substantive issues to ensure lasting peace and mutual understanding.

Ted Gurr, conflict analyst, contends that conflict management strategies that fail to recognize the importance of people's cultural identities or that fail to address the grievances that animate their political movements, will fail to reduce conflict.[105] Gurr shares an example of the Romani people. European governments have attempted to improve the status of the Roma by emphasizing protection of their civil and political rights; however, the enduring issues are based upon cultural discrimination. The plight of the Roma is unlikely to change until cultural differences are confronted, not by policies of assimilation but of pluralistic coexistence.[106]

---

102 Janice Gross Stein , "Image, Identity, and Conflict Resolution" in Chester A. Crocker, Fen Osler Hampson with Pamele Aall, *Managing Global Conflict: Sources of and Responses to International Conflict*, Washington, D.C.: United States Institute of Peace Press, 1996, p. 94-95.
103 Ibid, p.94-95.
104 Ibid, p. 98.
105 Ted Gurr, "Minorities, Nationalists, and Conflict" in Chester A. Crocker, Fen Osler Hampson with Pamela Aall, *Managing Global Conflict: Sources of and Responses to International Conflict*, Washington, D.C.: United States Institute of Peace Press, 1996. p. 66.
106 Ibid.

The roots of the conflict exist in the hearts and minds of the people, · not in the policy decision of diplomats. Only when the will of the people changes will politicians truly begin to listen. The Internet provides the potential in some environments for unparalleled reach.

Approaches

Renowned theorist and practitioner John Lederach argues that peace-building is fundamentally rooted in the building of relationships and trust. Lederach's position represents a paradigmatic shift away from a concern with the resolution of issues towards a frame of reference that focuses on the restoration and rebuilding of relationships.[107] Lederach encourages a focus on middle-level dialogue, versus a top-level or bottom-level dialogue, among communal groups rather than politicians or diplomats.

Lederach asserts that conflict transformation must be rooted in social-psychological and spiritual dimensions, which have been traditionally viewed as outside of scope of international diplomacy.[108] According to Lederach, an important meeting point between realism and innovation is the idea of reconciliation. The notion of reconciliation is that of a social space, where people and things come together.[109] During the experience of reconciliation, people are called upon to encounter themselves and their enemies, their hopes and their fears, and to acknowledge the past while envisioning the future.[110] Lederach stresses the importance of disengaging or minimizing conflicting group affiliations by engaging the sides as humans-in-relationship and facilitating opportunities for interdependence.

Of primary concern to Lederach is the fundamental question of how to create a sustainable catalyst for reconciliation in divided societies. Both conceptually and practically, Lederach feels that applications for reconciliation are still in their infancy. [111]

Theoretically, the idea of creating perpetual space for ongoing communication, reconciliation, and relationship building, as well as opportunities

---

107 John Paul Lederach, *Building Peace: Sustainable Reconciliation in Divided Societies*, Washington, D.C.: United States Institute of Peace Press, 1997, p. 24.
108 Ibid. p.60.
109 Ibid. p. 29.
110 Ibid. p.183.
111 Ibid, p.31.

for interdependence among disparate groups, is well suited for Internet applications involving reframing through relational diplomacy.

Intergroup Cohesion and Contagion

Ted Gurr contends that cohesive groups are those held together by dense networks of communication and interaction."[112] As peacebuilders strive to foster understanding, cooperation, and cohesion among conflicting parties, theories about intergroup cohesion provide important insights.

According to Gurr, cohesion is impaired in groups that have competing leaders and political movements. Effective intergroup mobilization in divided groups often depends on the formation of coalitions among diverse segments and contending leaders.[113] Failure to form coalitions reduces the scope and political impact of collective action and makes it easier for states to co-opt or ignore ethnopolitical challenges."[114]

One of the success stories of peacebuilders in Cyprus was their ability to form bicommunal coalitions of the willing. Many of these bicommunal groups were organized and maintained primarily through cyberspace. By weaving intergroup relationships, peacebuilders were able to mobilize diverse populations for collective action.

Contagion refers to the processes by which one group's actions provide inspiration and guidance, both strategic and tactical, for groups elsewhere.[115] Networks of communication allow groups to acquire better techniques for effective mobilization: plausible appeals, good leadership, and organizational skills. Groups also gain inspiration and encouragement from the successes of others. [116]

In Cyprus, bicommunal groups form a constellation of peacebuilders connected by the Internet. Successes of one group, through Internet

---

112 Ted Gurr, "Minorities, Nationalists, and Conflict" in Chester A. Crocker, Fen Osler Hampson with Pamela Aall, *Managing Global Conflict: Sources of and Responses to International Conflict*, Washington, D.C.: United States Institute of Peace Press, 1996, p. 66.

113 Ibid., p.14

114 Ibid.

115 Ted Gurr, "Minorities, Nationalists, and Conflict" in Chester A. Crocker, Fen Osler Hampson with Pamela Aall, *Managing Global Conflict: Sources of and Responses to International Conflict*, Washington, D.C: United States Institute of Peace Press, 1996, p. 66.

116 Ibid., p. 14

communications, quickly motivate other groups. This type of momentum is essential to sway both public and political opinion.

Change of Perceptions

"In both enduring interstate rivalries and bitter ethnic conflict, interests are shaped by images, which are in turn partially shaped by identity. What we see as a threat is a function in large part of the way we see the world and who we think we are."[117]

–Janice Stein

"In his brilliant analysis, Benedict Anderson observed that nations, unlike families and clans where individuals can know the others, are "imagined communities," whose past, tradition, and connections are interpreted and reinterpreted through time. Political identities similarly depend on imagined communities whose traditions are constructed and reinterpreted. Identities can therefore be shaped and reconfigured as leaders and communities restructure their relationships."[118]

–John Lederach

If the roots of conflict are intimately rooted in the cultural and psychological elements, which drive and sustain the conflict, what theoretical alternatives exist to change perceptions?

Janice Stein asserts that change in images is partly a function of the rate at which discrepant information occurs. According to cognitive psychologists, change in beliefs can occur rapidly with a gush of contradictory data or incrementally over time as people slowly incorporate information about their adversary, which is inconsistent with their previous knowledge.[119] As information flows become more open, images of the "other" gradually

---

117 Janice Gross Stein , "Image, Identity, and Conflict Resolution" in Chester A. Crocker, Fen Osler Hampson with Pamele Aall, *Managing Global Conflict: Sources of and Responses to International Conflict*, Washington, D.C.: United States Institute of Peace Press, 1996, p. 105.

118 John Paul Lederach, *Building Peace: Sustainable Reconciliation in Divided Societies*. Washington, D.C.: United States Institute of Peace Press, 1997, p. 106.

119 Janice Gross Stein , "Image, Identity, and Conflict Resolution" in Chester A. Crocker, Fen Osler Hampson with Pamele Aall, *Managing Global Conflict: Sources of and Responses to International Conflict*, Washington, D.C.: United States Institute of Peace Press, 1996, p. 99

begin to change.[120] By slowly redefining hostile imagery and underlying assumptions of "the other," conflict begins to slowly transform.[121] This process or learning about "the other" must also be reciprocated.[122]

Conflicting groups must make themselves part of a greater whole and learn to cooperate with "the other" towards mutually beneficial goals. Peacebuilders must consider both shocks and gradual persuasion in their repertoire. Creative marketing campaigns should also be considered. Lessons from the corporate world, including media blitzes, can be utilized to rebrand the humanity of "the other." The organization, Seeds of Peace, presents personal stories and profiles of "the other" online to create a more gradual shifting of perceptions. Internet marketing and advertising can be used by peacebuilders in the branding process.

Bottom-up Approach

There is a growing appreciation for the power of citizen diplomacy. This is sometimes referred to a bottom-up process versus a top-down or macro-level process.

John Prendergrast and Emily Plumb make a call for stronger recognition for the role of civil society and grassroots peacebuilding activities:

> "Peace implementation has mostly concerned itself with national-level peace agreements, international interventions, and peacekeeping forces. We argue that in order for peace agreements between warring parties to lead to durable peace, there needs to be, alongside top-down implementation of the peace agreement, concurrent bottom-up processes aimed at constructing a new social contract and healing societal divisions. Civil Society Organizations (CSOs) can have an impact through creating or supporting these

---

120   Ibid., p. 99
121   Eileen Babbitt and Tamra Pearson D'Estree , "An Israeli-Palestinian Women's Workshop: Application of the Interactive", in Chester A. Crocker, Fen Osler Hampson with Pamela Aall, *Managing Global Conflict: Sources of and Responses to International Conflict*, Washington, D.C: United States Institute of Peace Press, 1996, p. 528.
122   Janice Gross Stein , "Image, Identity, and Conflict Resolution" in Chester A. Crocker, Fen Osler Hampson with Pamele Aall, *Managing Global Conflict: Sources of and Responses to International Conflict*, Washington, D.C.: United States Institute of Peace Press, 1996, p.106.

bottom-up processes and through engendering societal ownership of the peace agreement."[123]

By building intercommunal links, initiating dialogue, and engaging people traditionally left out of the process, CSOs bring war-torn societies closer to reconciliation.[124]

As indicated, John Lederach promotes the idea of a middle-out process in which influential parties with direct or indirect links to top-level policy makers as well as wide public audiences, act as the primary catalysts by participating in various peacebuilding activities, including conflict resolution training programs.

The January demonstrations of over 70,000 people in Northern Nicosia, organized by non-state actors primarily through e-mail and cell phone messaging, inevitably had a powerful influence upon the political elites in Northern Cyprus. These demonstrations surely helped build the momentum for peacebuilders on both sides of the green line.

The cause and effect of each one of these steps cannot be measured, but these initiatives surely motivated, in part, the political decision-makers to allow bicommunal access on April 23, 2003. These demonstrations illustrate the power of the people, supported by technology, to make an even greater difference.

Interactive Dialogue

Diplomat Cameron Hume suggests: "We need to bring protagonists into a dialogue. Whether they are in conflict over dividing a state or deciding who rules, dialogue is essential. We also need a common vision. Dialogue must serve to change the way protagonists see their options. Antagonistic, mutually exclusive views of the future must yield to a common vision. It is precisely this sort of change that is transforming South African relations." [125]

---

123   John Prendergrast and Emily Plumb , "Building Local Capacity: From Implementation to Peacebuilding", in Stephen Stedman, Donald Rotchild and Elizabeth Cousens, *Enging Civil Wars,* Lynne Rienner, 2002, p. 327.
124   Ibid., p. 328.
125   Cameron Hume, "A Diplomat's View," in William Zartman, J. Lewis Rasmussen, *Peacemaking in International Conflict: Methods and Techniques*, Washington, D.C.: United States Institute of

When conflicts involve deep seeded animosity among the citizens of the opposing groups, it is the hearts and minds of the populace which must change. Who then should come into dialogue if not the masses? The governments as representatives of the people will only truly be motivated to change when the voices of the people resound. How can dialogue of such scale expect to be facilitated if not through technology, namely the Internet?

Peace Press, 1997, p. 319.

INTERCULTURAL COMMUNICATIONS & CULTURAL ADAPTATION THEORY

It logically follows that, in today's multicultural world, the truly reliable path to coexistence, to peaceful coexistence and creative cooperation, must start from what is at the root of all cultures and what lies infinitely deeper in human hearts and minds than political opinion. It must be rooted in self-transcendence. Transcendence as a hand reached out to those close to us, to foreigners, to the human community, to all living creatures, to nature, to the universe, transcendence as a deeply and joyously experienced need to be in harmony even with what we ourselves are not, what we do not understand, what seems distant from us in time and space, but with which we are nevertheless mysteriously linked because, together with us, all this constitutes a single world. Transcendence as the only real alternative to extinction.[126]

–President Vaclav Havel of the Czech Republic

In areas such as Cyprus, where divides exist along ethnic lines, important lessons may be drawn from intercultural communications and cultural adaptation theory. One of the major objectives of intercultural adaptation theory is to become intercultural—to transcend the "us" versus "them" paradigm in order to join a greater whole, in which independent parts coexist in harmony within a greater ring of cooperation and understanding. Each independent unit is able to successfully coexist through a greater understanding of "the other."

---

126   Young Yun Kim, *Becoming Intercultural: An Integrative Theory of Communication and Cross-Cultural Adaptation*, London: Sage Publications, 2001, p. 235.

In a sense, this strategy for coping with "the other" resembles the integrative-style of bargaining in which the pie is expanded to accommodate the diverse interests of all parties. Similarly, the conventional practice of exclusive ethnic loyalty with inherent disregard for "the other" resembles a positional bargaining tug of war in which one party usually feels cheated or at a loss.

Professor Young Yun Kim provides the following assumptions for cross-cultural adaptation in intercultural communications theory:

1. Humans are assumed to have an innate drive and capacity to adapt and grow.
2. Adaptation of an individual to a cultural environment occurs in and through communication.
3. Adaptation is a complex and dynamic process that brings about a qualitative transformation of the individual.[127]

Successful adaptation requires an affirmative attitude and willingness to change that lends itself to working with the host environment, not against it. This means striving to minimize the "us-versus-them" psychological orientation—a fundamental aspect of intercultural training.[128] Technology, if in the right hands, provides a medium to share motivational messages to encourage the need for positive change.

According to Dr. Kim, not all layers and facets of the environment are equally receptive, therefore it is important to reach out to those places, groups, and individuals that are particularly open and accessible, including local colleges, schools, businesses, civic organizations, churches, and other public and private entities. The Internet is an effective arena in which to build diverse coalitions of the willing and also to find others with similar interests and ideas.

According to Dr. Kim, "There may be ongoing programs such as "host families" and "buddy systems" that provide opportunities to interact and engage in interpersonal relationships. We facilitate our own successful

---

127 Young Yun Kim, *Becoming Intercultural: An Integrative Theory of Communication and Cross-Cultural Adaptation*, London: Sage Publications, 2001, p. 88.
128 Ibid., p. 224.

adaptation by going beyond our ethnic community and reaching out for opportunities to participate in the interpersonal and mass communications processes of the host milieu."[129]

The Internet provides a platform for powerful communications and introduction tools. Nicos Anastasiou has worked on a matching service, similar in concept to the "buddy system" referred to by Dr. Kim. A buddy system matches people across conflict lines who have similar interests, such as writing, art, music, photography, cooking, etc. In recent days, we have experienced a proliferation of "matchmaking" websites. This concept is similar in nature, but with a focus on building interpersonal relationships among conflicting groups.

The power of the Internet to assist in the forming of human relationships should not be overlooked.

---

129 Young Yun Kim, *Becoming Intercultural: An Integrative Theory of Communication and Cross-Cultural Adaptation*, London: Sage Publications, 2001, p. 225.

SOCIOLOGICAL CONSIDERATIONS

Interdependence

Interdependence is the core component of social life. According to Sociologist Susan Fiske, "It glues together dyadic relationships, defines psychological groups, structures organizations, predicts the content of group stereotypes, and determines intergroup relations. Having outcomes contingent on another person motivates understanding that other person in the service of prediction and control." [130]

As we have witnessed, technology can be used to create joint bicommunal projects among diverse groups, even among populations in diaspora. Peace-Cyprus.org is an example of bicommunal interdependence and cooperation.

Increasing Contact

Producing more individualized perceptions of outgroup members and more personalized relationships can help reduce bias. [131]

Dual Identification

The idea of dual identification is based on the recognition that social identities with different groups at different levels of inclusiveness need not be mutually exclusive. More specifically, it assumes that individuals can have strong attachment to a specific subgroup and at the same time identify with a superordinate group. Dual identification is presumed to mitigate

---

130 Susan T. Fiske, "Interdependence and the Reduction of Prejudice," in Stuart Oskamp, ed., *Reducing Prejudice and Discrimination*, London : Lawrence Erlbaum Associates, 2000, p. 117.

131 John Dovidio, Kerry Kawakami, and Samuel Gaertner, "Reducing Contemporary Prejudice: Combating Explicit and Implicit Bias at the Individual and Intergroup Level", in Stuart Oskamp, ed., *Reducing Prejudice and Discrimination* , London : Lawrence Erlbaum Associates , 2000, p. 158.

the negative effects of ingroup-outgroup comparisons. Dual identities in this sense have been promoted as an appropriate model for multiethnic societies, allowing for preservation of ethnic differentiation and ethnic identity on the one hand, and integration at the national level on the other.[132] This type of categorization creates cross-cutting distinctions, which makes social categorization more complex and reduces the magnitude of ingroup-outgroup distinctions. [133]

Acceptance of the "Other"

The process of acceptance may be defined as relationships becoming more and more caring and committed as proximity and interaction continue. The process of acceptance begins with positive interdependence. Individuals must believe that they "sink or swim" in striving to achieve important mutual goals. Striving for mutual benefit requires promotive interaction—assisting, helping, sharing, and encouraging each other's efforts to achieve. More promotive interaction among individuals leads to greater resulting interpersonal attraction. [134]

Cooperative situations, in contrast, generate a multidimensional, dynamic, and realistic view of others. Negative stereotypes tend to lose their primary potency and to be reduced when interactions reveal enough detail that group members are seen as individuals rather than as members of an ethnic group. All collaborators become "one of us." In other words, cooperation widens the sense of who is in the group, and "they" become "we."[135]

Prejudice Results from Threat

Some theorists argue that prejudice stems from the need to maintain self-esteem and that derogation of the outgroup serves to maintain ingroup

---

132 Marilynn Brewer, "Reducing Prejudice Through Cross-Categorization: Effects of Multiple Social Identities", in Stuart Oskamp, ed., *Reducing Prejudice and Discrimination* , London : Lawrence Erlbaum Associates , 2000, p. 169.
133 Ibid.
134 Ibid.
135 Ibid., p. 247.

self-value. Strategies to reduce prejudice include raising the self-esteem or affirming the central values of the ingroup.[136]

Prejudice from Perceived Differences

Other theorists posit that prejudice is a consequence of perceiving others as different from oneself or one's group. Theories suggest that prejudice may be reduced by highlighting a superordinate goal or attempting to display signs and symbols that emphasize or create a shared identity between the target and the prejudiced perceiver, because this shared identity will minimize perceived differences. [137] Author Dr. Parekh refers to finding commonality in multicultural societies:

> "Like any other society, a multicultural society needs a broadly shared culture to sustain it. Since it involves several cultures, the shared culture can only grow out of their interaction and should both respect and nurture their diversity and unite them around a common way of life. For those accustomed to thinking of culture as a more or less homogeneous and coherent whole, the idea of multiculturally constituted culture might appear incoherent or bizarre. In fact, such a culture is a fairly common phenomenon in every culturally diverse society."[138]

As Nicos Anastasiou stressed, there is a common Cypriot culture, such as a Cypriot dance and common words among the languages. Peacebuilders are working hard to foster pride in a shared heritage, while instilling respect and appreciation for differences.

---

136 Brenda Major, Wendy Quinton, Shannon McCoy, and Toni Schmader, "Reducing Prejudice: The Target's Perspective," in Stuart Oskamp, ed., *Reducing Prejudice and Discrimination* , London : Lawrence Erlbaum Associates , 2000, p. 220.
137 Ibid., p. 222-223.
138 Peter Kivisto, *21ˢᵗ Century Sociology: Multiculturalism in a Global Society*, Oxford: Blackwell Publishing, 2002, p. 36.

PUBLIC DIPLOMACY: LESSONS
FOR PEACEBUILDERS

We cannot gauge our success by sales. No profit and loss statement sums up our operations at the end of each year. No cash register rings when a man changes his mind, no totals are rung up on people impressed with an idea. There is no market listing of the rise or fall in the going rate of belief in an ideal. Often, one's best work may be merely to introduce doubt into the minds already firmly committed.

–Edward R. Murrow, U.S. Information Agency Director (USIA),
1961-1964[139]

No one of the U.S. Information Agency's various information activities, or all or them together, can be expected to bring about sudden and dramatic changes in our international relations. Eventually, however, a consistent, conscientious information and cultural program—fair and accurate reporting of the American scene—will surely bring about greater understanding in the world community. This in turn can contribute to better political and diplomatic relations.

–George V. Allen, U.S. Information Agency Director (USIA),
1957-1960[140]

Public diplomacy offers valuable lessons to peacebuilders. Creative technological applications will further empower peacebuilders to broaden their reach. Until integrated with the US State Department in 1999, the United States Information Agency (USIA) was responsible for public

---

139   *The United States Information Agency: A Commemoration*, Published by the USIA, p.30.

140   *The United States Information Agency: A Commemoration*, Published by the USIA, p.21.

diplomacy in the United States. The USIA offers the following definition: Public diplomacy seeks to promote the national interest and the national security of the United States through understanding, informing, and influencing foreign publics and broadening dialogue between American citizens and institutions and their counterparts abroad.

Some of the varied projects of the USIA include: US book translation projects in scores of foreign languages with over 190 million copies distributed since 1950; cultural exhibits and world fairs; student exchanges (Fulbright Program); science, technology, athletics, research, culture, and performing arts exchanges; cultural magazine publications, including USIA's monthly magazine, *Free World*; influential movie production; entertainment propaganda, including drama teams; Voice of America and other media-related endeavors; US product promotion; artist ambassadors program; disinformation response; and English language training.[141]

In 1997, the USIS Nicosia (branch of the USIA) and the Cyprus Fulbright Commission provided a diverse range of creative initiatives, including: host lectures, workshops, art exhibits, concerts, conferences, festivals, summer camps, bicommunal International Visitor Tours—the full chest of public diplomacy tools brought to bear to promote peace on a citizen-to-citizen level. According to Judith Baroody, Foreign Service Office, "These activities catalyzed others carried out by the Cypriots themselves, a chain reaction that led to over 600 bicommunal events by the end of that year. Activities included one-on-one encounters to a fair that brought over 4,000 Cypriots together in the buffer zone."[142]

As the gates closed in 1997, the USIS and the Fulbright Commission continued to toil to create opportunities for intercommunal dialogue though the Internet, a joint magazine, and off-island workshops. Baroody recalls, "In teaching by example, the USIS and Fulbright staffs provided a model of what the people of Cyprus could achieve by crossing through the barbed wire barrier—physical, political and psychological—to work together for peace."[143]

---

141 *The United States Information Agency: A Commemoration*, Published by the USIA, p.1-80.
142 *The United States Information Agency: A Commemoration*, Published by the USIA, p. 66.
143 *The United States Information Agency: A Commemoration*, Published by the USIA, p. 66.

Public diplomacy programs, as performed by the USIA, offer a plethora of creative ideas to peacebuilders. The Internet provides a unique vehicle to facilitate public diplomacy among relational diplomats, expand reach, and connect vast populations. The Internet can be used to foster online and off-line cultural exchanges.

The Internet is also a powerful media tool. The Voice of America was one of the USIA's most powerful vehicles of persuasion and influence. The Internet provides options for audio (radio, educational, entertainment), visual (movies, dramas, news, short films, cultural presentations), and text-based mass media appeals (news and magazine sites, email mailers, and online communities).

According to David Hitchcock at the Center for Strategic International Studies, "Public diplomacy can be greatly aided by civic and international exchange activities of the private sector. Although State and USIA are already quite involved, more can be done."[144]

---

144 David I. Hitchcock, Jr., *U.S. Public Diplomacy* , Washington, D.C. : The Center for Strategic and International Studies, Volume X, Number 17, p. 9.

CYPRUS AFTER APRIL 23, 2003

On April 23, 2003, for the first time in nearly 30 years, the Turkish Cypriots eased border restrictions and opened the Ledra Palace checkpoint in Nicosia along the dividing green line. The opening of the border came one week after Greek Cypriots signed the EU accession treaty. After the UN-sponsored peace plan was rejected by Turkish Cypriot leader Rauf Denktas in March 2003, both sides engaged in a series of confidence-building measures. Serdar Denktas, the deputy Turkish Cypriot prime minister and son of the president, said the easing of restrictions would be a test of whether the two sides could live together: "This is a unilateral decision passed to build confidence and promote peace." [145]

After the move by Turkish Cypriots to relax border controls, Greek officials announced a further series of confidence-building measures. Turkish Cypriots were allowed to trade in the South and gain access to healthcare and other state benefits available to Greek Cypriots. Efforts were also be made to improve educational ties between North and South and to restore telephone connections. There was even an invitation to Turkish Cypriots to join the Cypriot Olympic Team in 2004. [146]

After April 23, 2003 more border checkpoints were opened and hundreds of thousands of people have crossed sides. Throughout 2003, international sanctions were held in place and the EU demanded that unless unification was achieved in time for formal EU membership by May 2004, only the Greek side would be granted admission. [147]

---

145 BBC News UK Edition, "Emotion as Cyprus border opens", http://news.bbc.co.uk/1/hi/world/europe/2969089.stm, April 23, 2003.
146 BBC News UK Edition, "Cyprus trade ban lifted", http://news.bbc.co.uk/1/hi/world/europe/2989873.stm, April 30, 2003.
147 BBC News UK Edition, "Emotion as Cyprus border opens", http://news.bbc.co.uk/1/hi/world/europe/2969089.stm, April 23, 2003.

The entire island entered the EU on May 1, 2004, although the EU acquis - the body of common rights and obligations - applies only to the areas under the internationally recognized Greek Cypriot Government, and is suspended in the areas administered by Turkish Cypriots. However, individual Turkish Cypriots able to document their eligibility for Republic of Cyprus citizenship legally enjoy the same rights accorded to other citizens of European Union states.

These were certainly welcoming signs, but Kofi Annan of the United Nations warned that there was no substitute for a comprehensive settlement.[148] Nevertheless, peacebuilders in Cyprus were quite enthusiastic about events. Many friends on both sides of the green line were able to meet in person.

Co-founder of Tech4Peace.org, Dr. Laouris comments, "Since April 23, there is freedom of movement, which is revolutionary for Cyprus. But the system of online peacebuilding is not outdated because freedom of movement doesn't mean interaction. It doesn't mean that people share what experiences they had."[149] The Internet will continue to enhance communications. Dr. Laouris noted that there has always been an increase in Internet activity when people are able to meet and there is more going on.[150] Now that the borders are open, the Internet and technology will perhaps become an even more dynamic tool for peacebuilders in different ways.

Eser Keskiner, co-founder of Peace-Cyprus.org reiterates the continued role of technology, "Still technology, in terms of getting the news out, is a major thing. For example, anything that happens in Cyprus, within a few hours, we can just publicize it all over the world, which is what the Internet brought to the world in general. But other than that, the Internet is going to keep its role as where all the resources are kept open to the public and in terms of keeping the debate public as well. So basically, the main contribution of technology, as I see it, is still taking all the initiatives out of a group of elites and bring them to the public domain."[151]

148 Country profile: Cyprus, BBC News UK Edition, http://news.bbc.co.uk/1/hi/world/europe/country_profiles/1016541.stm, June 8, 2003
149 Interview with Dr. Yiannis Laouris, Co-founder of Tech4Peace.org, June 2003
150 Ibid.
151 Interview with Eser Keskiner, Co-founder of Peace-Cyprus.org, May 2003.

The border opening has facilitated the use of previously restricted meeting as well. TV and radio are now being used more than ever to publicly bring people together from both sides. Peacebuilders, such as Nicos Anastasiou, recognize the new power of TV and radio as a way for bicommunal groups to share their messages.

As there is greater interaction, there is also a greater risk for attacks. Dr. Benjamin Broome believes that peacebuilding efforts will perhaps be even more important with greater integration.[152] The Internet, as a tool to build bridges, organize, and inform, will clearly continue to play an important role. As intercommunal networks expand, the Internet will also play a vital role as a creative incubator.

The election of a new Cypriot president in 2008 served as the impetus for the UN to encourage both the Turkish and Cypriot Governments to reopen unification negotiations. In September 2008, the leaders of the Greek Cypriot and Turkish Cypriot communities started negotiations under UN auspices aimed at reuniting the divided island.

---

152 Interview with Dr. Benjamin Broome, Professor of Communications, Arizona State University and Former US Fulbright Scholar to Cyprus, February 2003.

CONCLUSION

The enormity of the peacebuilding task, particularly in deeply divided societies, requires a multi-dimensional approach to peacebuilding. Peacebuilders of all walks of life, professional and citizen, young and old, must recognize their role as relational diplomats and venture boldly into new territory in the conquest for peace.

On a grassroots level, relational diplomacy can inspire the massive societal shifts required to create lasting change. As Internet usage and mobile phone technologies continue to proliferate worldwide, technology offers unprecedented opportunities for instantaneous communications and expansive collaboration. As we have witnessed in Cyprus, there have been successful programs implementing creative technologies to foster peace, but the true potential of the technological domain remains untapped.

The events of January 2011 in the Jasmine Revolution in Tunisia provide further evidence of the power of technology in supporting grassroots movements. On January 14, 2011, a sudden wave of street protests led authoritarian president, Zine el-Abidine Ben Ali, to flee Tunisia after having ruled with an iron fist for 23 years. It is unlikely that the Jasmine Revolution would have been successful in ousting the president if technology had not been used so effectively in the hands of the masses.

In Egypt, President Hosni Mubarak was forced to step down after 18 days of civil unrest and protests during the Egyptian Revolution which started on January 25, 2011. On January 28, 2011, President Mubarak, recognizing the power of cell phones and social media, tried to silence the protestors by shutting down his country's access to the Internet. Despite his efforts, the Internet ban only lasted five days and Mubarak resigned on February 11, 2011. Elsewhere, in the Middle East from Libya to Syria, Bahrain and beyond, the prodigious use of technology has fueled protests and revolutions by empowering the masses to connect and make their resounding voices heard.

Suspicion of the role of technology in peacebuilding by professional practitioners must not hinder our efforts to be highly proactive in the pursuit of innovative initiatives using technology for peace. Surely not a panacea for global conflict, technology has an important role to play, especially when combined with traditional forms of Track I and II diplomacy

The hard-earned experiences and dynamic strategies of peacebuilders in Cyprus provide invaluable insights and clues to conflictants in other troubled parts of the world. When broken down to the common denominator, it is the relational diplomats–the people on the streets–who control the fate of peace. If given the proper tools, these relational diplomats–these everyday citizens–can be empowered to realize the peace that they so desperately seek.

APPENDICES

Appendix A: Overview of Conflict Resolution Activities in Cyprus

The arrow should be interpreted as "Made Possible" or
"Laid the Groundwork For" the subsequent phases. (Benjamin Broome)

Phase V: Local Initiatives in Conflict Resolution (1995-1997)
- Agora/Bazaar to form 15 bicommunal project teams, 1995.
- Special projects (e.g. music concerts) and study groups.
- Ongoing meetings & workshops for educators, citizens groups, management trainees, and others 1995-1997.
- Pivotal Ledra Palace gathering after August events, 1996.
- Conflict Resolution Skills Training workshops for university students, 1997.
- Workshops in Turkish Cypriot community for various groups (e.g. women's organizations), 1996-1997.
- Presentations, exhibitions, and workshops in Greek Cypriot community by Peace Center, 1994-1997.
- Training for groups outside Cyprus (Israeli-Palestinian group, Irish group, London Cypriots), 1997. Internet Project, *Hade* Magazine, co-villager visits, youth encounters, environmentalists, and others, 1997.

Phase IV: Interactive Design and Problem Solving Workshops (1994-1997)

(see Broome, 1996; Broome, in press)

- Nine month series of weekly design sessions on peacebuilding efforts in Cyprus, 1994-1995 (G/C & T/C "Problematiques," Collective Vision Statement, Collaborative Action Agenda.
- Ongoing design workshops held with young business leaders, young political leaders, university students, and women's groups, 1995-1996.
- Design workshop with G/C, T/C, Greek & Turkish peacebuilders, Les Diablerets, Switzerland, 1997. Interactive Management Training Workshop, 1997.

Phase III: Training Program in Conflict Resolution (1991-1997)
(see Diamond & Fisher, 1995)

- Series of mini-workshops on conflict resolution in Niocosia, 1991 & 1992 (Diamond)
- Ten day workshops in Oxford, England, 1993 (IMTD).
- Bi-Communal Steering Committee formed, 1993 (IMTD).
- Six 7 day workshops held in U.S. and Nicosia, 1994 (Cyprus Consortium).

  Five 7 day workshops held in U.S. and Nicosia, 1995-1997 (Cyprus Consortium).

Phase II: Citizen-Organized Bicommunal Contacts (1989-1991)
(see Hadjipavlou-Trigeorgis, 1993)

- Local Steering Committee formed by participants in Berlin workshop, 1989.
- Bi-Communal meetings and conflict resolution workshops at Ledra Palace, 1990.
- Citizens Movement for Democracy and Federation in Cyprus formed, 1990.
- Joint art exhibits, music concerts, and poetry evenings, 1990 & 1991.

⇧

Phase I: Periodic Third-Party Problem Solving Workshops (1996-1993)

- One 5-day workshop for high-level representatives from London, 1966 (Burton).
- One 5-day workshop for political leaders in Rome, 1973 (Talbot).
- Series of meetings for intellectuals in Nicosia ("Operation Locksmith"), 1985 (Doob).
- Two weekend workshops at Harvard, 1979 & 1984 (Kelman).
- Two 4-day workshops for educators in Nicosia, 1993 (Fisher).

Appendix B: Overview of 15 Peacebuilding Projects of Agora/Bazaar (Benjamin Broome)

Between fall of 1994 and summer of 1995, a core group of thirty-two Greek Cypriot and Turkish Cypriot conflict resolution trainers and project leaders participated in problem-solving and design sessions focused on peace-building efforts in Cyprus. Groups met on a weekly basis, and occasionally on weekends, both in separate community meetings and in bi-communal settings. A group design process called Interactive Management was used to guide the groups through three phases of problem solving: definition of the situation, vision of the future, and development of a strategic set of projects for promoting peace-building activities in Cyprus.

In the first phase of group work, each community worked separately to identify the obstacles to their work and to structure these into a Problématique, or system of problems, surrounding the peace-building process. In the second phase, participants again worked in separate community groups to construct vision statements for their peace-building efforts, and they came together in a bi-communal setting to construct a collective vision statement. In the third phase, during which all sessions were bi-communal, participants proposed a total of 241 possible projects designed to work toward their vision, and they eventually selected 15 of these projects for implementation during the following year. They held an Agora/bazaar to which they invited others who had expressed interest in joining them in peace building efforts (Benjamin Broome).

#	PROJECT
1	Form study groups on Cyprus Federation/EU
2	Establish regular columns in G/C and T/C newspapers by members of opposite community
3	Schedule series of lectures by Orthodox and Muslim priests
4	Establish bi-communal meetings for T/Cs and G/Cs who studied together in integrated schools before 1974 (English School and American Academy)
5	Find sponsors for publishing books on poetry, short stories, art, folk dances in both languages

6   Establish a bi-communal womens research center and support group
7   Form a bi-communal research center on history, social structure, traditions, culture, oral history of the two communities
8   Conduct bi-communal workshops for young political leaders
9   Establish bi-communal center to teach internet and Greek and Turkish languages
10 Organize bi-communal workshops on problem solving techniques for educationalists
11 Set up bi-communal training/research center on conflict resolution and problem solving
12 Create bi-communal dialogue groups to focus on critical issues (property concerns, identity, security, etc.)
13 Organize poetry evenings for bi-communal audience
14 Organize concert with theme Peace on the Green Line
15 Study the living conditions of T/Cs who live in the South and G/Cs who live in the North and make joint public report

Appendix C: Timeline: Cyprus Chronology of Key Events

1914 - Cyprus annexed by Britain, after more than 300 years of Ottoman rule.

1925 - Becomes crown colony.

1955 - Greek Cypriots begin guerrilla war against British rule. The guerrilla movement, the National Organization of Cypriot Combatants (EOKA), wants enosis (unification) with Greece.

1956 - Archbishop Makarios, head of enosis campaign, deported to the Seychelles.

1959 - Archbishop Makarios returns and is elected President.

1960 - Cyprus gains independence after Greek and Turkish communities reach agreement on a constitution. Britain retains sovereignty over two military bases.

1963 - Makarios raises Turkish fears by proposing constitutional changes which would abrogate power-sharing arrangements. Intercommunal violence erupts. Turkish side withdraws from power sharing.

1964 - United Nations peacekeeping force set up.

1974 - Military junta in Greece backs coup against Makarios, who escapes. Within days Turkish troops land in the North to protect Turkish community, Greek Cypriots flee their homes. Coup collapses. Turkish forces occupy a third of the island, enforce partition between North and South. Glafkos Clerides, President of the House of Representatives, becomes President until Makarios returns in December.

1975 - Turkish Cypriots establish independent administration, with Rauf Denktas as President.

1977 - Makarios dies. Succeeded by Spyros Kyprianou.

1980 -UN-sponsored peace talks resume.

1983 - Denktas suspends talks and proclaims Turkish Republic of Northern Cyprus (TRNC). It is recognized only by Turkey.

1985 - No agreement at talks between Denktas and Kyprianou.

1988 - Georgios Vassiliou elected Greek Cypriot president.

1989 - Vassiliou-Denktas talks abandoned.

1992 - Talks resume and collapse again.

1993 - Glafkos Clerides replaces Vassiliou as president.

1994 - European Court of Justice rules that all direct trade between northern Cyprus and European Union is illegal.

1996 - Increased tension, violence along buffer zone.

1997 - Failure of UN-mediated peace talks between Clerides and Denktas.

1998 - Clerides re-elected to a second term by narrow margin. EU lists Cyprus as potential member. Clerides's government threatens to install Russian-made anti-aircraft missiles. Turkey threatens military action. Clerides decides not to deploy missiles in Cyprus.

2001 June - The UN Security Council renews its 36-year mission in Cyprus. Some 2,400 peacekeepers patrol the buffer zone between Greek and Turkish Cypriots. Turkey keeps 35,000 troops in the north.

2001 July - Dozens of police officers are injured as protesters attack a British military base at Akrotiri over plans to build telecommunications masts alleged to pose a health hazard.

2001 November - Turkey threatens to annex the north if the Republic of Cyprus joins the European Union before a settlement is reached.

2002 January - Clerides and Denktas begin UN-sponsored negotiations. Minds are concentrated by EU membership aspirations.

2002 November - UN Secretary General Kofi Annan presents a comprehensive peace plan for Cyprus which envisages a federation with two constituent parts, presided over by a rotating presidency.

2002 December - EU summit in Copenhagen invites Cyprus to join in 2004 provided the two communities agree to UN plan by early spring 2003. Without reunification, only the internationally recognized Greek Cypriot part of the island will gain membership.

2003 February - Tassos Papadopoulos defeats Clerides in presidential elections with just weeks to go before deadline for agreeing to the UN plan for the island's future.

2003 March - UN deadline for agreement on reunification plan passes without agreement. Secretary-General Kofi Annan acknowledges that the plan has failed.

2003 April 23 - Turkish and Greek Cypriots cross the island's dividing "green line" for the first time in 30 years, after the Turkish Cypriot authorities say they are easing restrictions to build confidence between the communities. Within three days some 17,000 people have made the crossing.

The following year in April 2004, Denktas loses his 30-year stronghold on power. Mehmet Ali Talat is elected as the new Turkist Cypriot prime minister. Talat, a more modern leader and head of the center-left Cumhuriyetçi Türk Partisi (CTP; Republican Turkish Party), supports unification and Kofi Annan's plan. The entire island entered the EU on May 1, 2004, although the EU acquis - the body of common rights and obligations - applies only to the areas under the internationally recognized Greek Cypriot Government, and is suspended in the areas administered by Turkish Cypriots. However, individual Turkish Cypriots able to document their eligibility for Republic of Cyprus citizenship legally enjoy the same rights accorded to other citizens of European Union states.

The election of a new left-wing Cypriot president, Dimitris Christofias, in 2008 served as the impetus for the UN to encourage both the Turkish and Cypriot Governments to reopen unification negotiations. In September 2008, the leaders of the Greek Cypriot and Turkish Cypriot communities started negotiations under UN auspices aimed at reuniting the divided island. The path to peace is long from over, but progress has been made, assisted largely by relational diplomats employing technological innovations.

Appendix D: Map of Partitioned Island of Cyprus

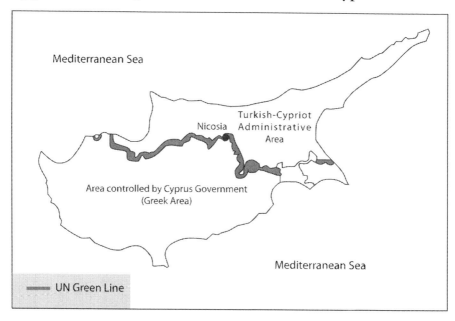

Appendix E: Map of Partitioned City of Nicosia

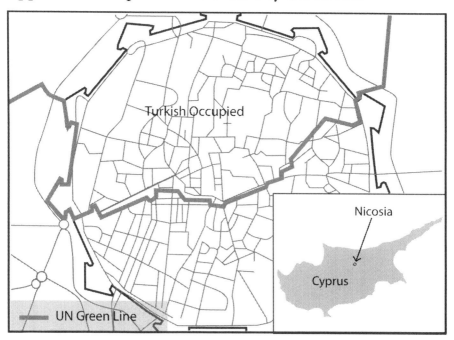

Appendix F: Nicos Anastasiou Newsletter Sample

— Original Message —
From: Nicos Anastasiou
Sent: Friday, June 27, 2003 12:48 PM
Subject: Are we Cinderellas?

Dear friends,

The amazing and powerful 'web' of citizens' contacts between the two sides continues getting bigger and stronger every day. Whatever the intentions of those who made the decision for this change, it seems to me, this is the best preparation that we could have for the real solution. This 'web' cannot be broken. The 'other side' of our country is not a 'tourist' destination where we go for curiosity. The people themselves are showing the way to the politicians. Some indications of the 'web':

a.. A G/C friend of mine from the co-villagers project just phoned up to say that his granddaughter is getting married in Limassol and that a group of 60 T/Cs from their old mixed village in the north will be coming to the south to celebrate with them.

b.. The G/Cs and T/Cs from the two sides of the checkpoint at Limnitis have been coordinating their efforts in the last few weeks to protest and request together that this particular checkpoint also is open. Similar efforts were made by the shopkeepers on both sides of Ledra Street in Nicosia.

c.. Despite the seemingly more 'normal' feeling, compared with the intensity of emotions when the checkpoints were first opened, the people crossing to the 'other side' are continuing to do so in their thousands (e.g. between 13 - 23 of June more than 110,000 people crossed; about equally divided between T/Cs and G/Cs).

There are many events being organised in the next few days that merit everyone's support. Let us join everywhere we can, celebrate together, fight together, forgive each other (reconciliation within groups, within communities, between parties or individuals is just as important as between the two communities).

Nicos
Common performance of the Bi-communal Choir and Steps for Peace in Limassol:
Medieval Castle, Saturday, 28 June, 8:30 pm

It was a dream that these two well known bi-communal groups had for a long time: To be able to perform anywhere in Cyprus together. The plans were made even before the loosening of the controls at the checkpoints. Members of the executive committees of the two groups worked 'blend' together the songs of the choir with the Cypriot dances of 'Steps for Peace' into a single programme. On Saturday night, they will be the guests of the mayor of Limassol, Mr. Kontides. The programme will also include readings of poetry and prose in Greek and Turkish written specifically for this event by George Sofocleous. Entrance is free.

Co-villagers' reunions: Petra, Elia, Angolemi, Ayios Georgios - Sunday, 29 June

Our co-villagers project of trying to bring together people from both communities who used to live in mixed villages continues this Sunday. More than one hundred G/Cs have already signed up and will be going to these villages in the Morfou area in the north part of Cyprus. Buses will be leaving from the Ledra Palace at 10:30 am and the village of Elia will be the place where everyone will eventually be meeting. Even if we have been doing this work for many years there is always great excitement and newfound hope when we make a new start with villages we did not cover before. We are hoping for a good media coverage, both local and international - a team from the National Geographic magazine will be with us on the day...

For new friends receiving this message who have not been following this project before here are some websites with some information on the co-villagers project:

http://www.peace-cyprus.org/VillagersMeeting/Louroujina/
http://www.peace-cyprus.org/VillagersMeeting/July1/
http://www.peacecyprus.org/VillagersMeeting/Paphos/
http://www.tech4peace.org/nqcontent.cfm?a_id=1737
http://arifler.mycyprus.net/english/Lurucina/reunion1/
jan272002.htm

a.. If you wish to arrange more such reunions of either one village or a cluster of villages in the north or south parts of Cyprus and would like our support or more information how to organise such events please send an e-mail.

"Solution Now" open meeting: Monday 30 June, Ledra Palace Hotel, 7:30 pm

This important bi-communal civil society initiative formed recently has the following aims as announced by the temporary committee:

- To build and promote an effective common Cypriot Movement.
- To form a civil society pressure group for the solution of the Cyprus problem.
- To promote the Anan plan for the solution of the Cyprus problem by May 2004.

The meeting on Monday is open to anyone to attend and in the agenda, among others, will be the group's five ongoing projects:

- Real life stories in the media
- 15th and 20th of July project
- Structuring of the movement

- Translation of public documents in Turkish
- Opinion poll on the Anan plan

Rhythm of Peace (YEP 14): The first multi-communal youth music competition – Press conference at Ledra Palace, Wednesday 2 July, 11:00 am

The 14th group of the Youth Encounters for Peace (YEP) project focuses its work on music as a means of making bridges of peace in Cyprus. The group is organising the first music competition for young musicians aiming to promote talented Cypriot musicians and create a platform where musicians from the communities of Cyprus can meet and collaborate. A press conference is being organised next Wednesday to announce the project to the general public.

The basic information:

a.. The competition is open to anyone aged 15 to 25.

b.. The competition will take place in the context of this year's celebrations of the Cyprus Day of Peace on the 30th of September (more on the other plans for the celebrations in a forthcoming message).

c.. There will be two parallel competitions: one for classical and one for contemporary music.

d.. Applicants must be groups of 2 to 5 persons (for the classical competition) or 2 or more (for contemporary music). The group may already exist or may be formed for the occasion.

e.. In each group there must be at least one G/C and one T/C. Members of the other communities of Cyprus are most welcome.

f.. Each group will perform one piece (or movement of a piece) of its own choice. Duration will be 6 to 10 minutes (classical music) or 5 to 6 minutes (contemporary music).

g.. A musician may participate in more than one group.

h.. For the contemporary music competition there is no restriction in the style of the music performed, although extreme styles are not encouraged.

i.. Before applying please consider that performances of at least semi-professional level are required.

j.. Any young musicians interested to take part but do not know any one from the 'other side' can say so in the application form and we shall bring them in contact with musicians of similar interests and type of music. For this purpose we will be building a data base to 'match' people so that groups can be formed that can take part in the competition.

k.. The organisers, if asked, will be providing advice regarding repertoire and also some coaching if necessary.

l.. During the day of the competition a piano will be provided for the classical music part.

m.. The contemporary music contestants will have a sound system provided.

n.. Deadline to receive applications is Saturday, 2 August, 2003. For more details and application forms contact:

PLEASE PASS ON THIS INFORMATION ABOUT THE COMPETI-TION TO ANY YOUNG MUSICIAN FRIENDS YOU MAY HAVE, MUSIC SCHOOLS AND MUSIC TEACHERS!!

The great concert of Maria Farantouri and Zulfu Livanelli: Friday, 4 July, D'
Avilla, Nicosia at 8:30 p.m.

Two of the most famous musicians of Greece and Turkey will be in Cyprus for a great concert next Friday. The organisers are the Cultural Office of AKEL, the Movement for Culture and the Bi-communal Choir. Doros Demosthenous, Erkan Dagli, the Bi-communal Choir and Steps for Peace will also make their own contributions to the programme. I hope that there will be a massive presence of the good people of Cyprus to celebrate together on Friday night.

"Hands Across the Divide" bi-communal women's group - protest against the use of passports at checkpoints: Wednesday, 9 July,

Ledra Palace checkpoints, from 7:00 p.m. till Midnight (Cinderella time!)

From the time the restrictions to movement were partially lifted there are some specific issues that many G/Cs and T/Cs have been feeling strongly about. Examples:

a.. Showing our passports at the checkpoints. Are we going to another country?

b.. Having to return back to 'our' side by midnight. Are we Cinderellas or what?

c.. The limited number of checkpoints that people can cross from. What about the others like in Dherinia or Limnitis?

Hands Across the Divide, this very active and inspiring women's group, has decided to do something about it. On the date and times above, they will be at the Ledra Palace checkpoints to protest on these issues. Their plans include having a huge clock, a Cinderella puppet, a fairy and a number of slogans. There will also be a text for people to sign as well as a book to write messages, etc.

And they are asking everyone's support! Let's be there!!

There is also a need for volunteers to help in making all the preparations for that day.

****

Nicos Anastasiou,

"We must combine the toughness of the serpent and the softness of the dove, a tough mind and a tender heart." Martin Luther King Jr.

BIBLIOGRAPHY

Mary B. Anderson, *Do No Harm: Supporting Local Capacities for Peace through Aid.* Cambridge, Mass.: Local Capacities for Peace Project/ Collaborative for Development Action, Inc., 1996.

Edward Azar, "The Analysis and Management of Protracted Conflict," in *The Psychodynamics of International Relationships,* Volume 2, by Vamik D. Volkan, Joseph V. Montville and Demetrios A. Julius, Lanham, MD: Lexington Books, 1991.

David Bell, *An Introduction to Cybercultures*, London: Routledge Group Press, 2001.

Benjamin J. Broome. "Overview of Conflict Resolution Activities in Cyprus: Their Contribution to the Peace Process." *The Cyprus Review*, 1997

Robert Burnett and David Marshall, *Web Theory*, London: Routledge Group Press, 2003.

Diana Chigas, Negotiating Intractable Conflicts: The Contributions of Unofficial Intermediaries, Draft in process of United States Institute of Peace, 2003

Chester A. Crocker, Fen Osler Hampson with Pamela Aall, *Managing Global Conflict: Sources of and Responses to International Conflict*, United States Institute of Peace Press: Washington, D.C. 1996.

Ronald J. Fisher, "Generic principles for resolving intergroup conflict", *Journal of Social Issues*, Plenum Publishing Corporation , Volume 50, Number 1, Spring 1994.

Maria Hadjipavlou-Trigeorgis. "Unofficial Inter-Communal Contacts and Their Contribution to Peacebuilding in Conflict Societies: The Case of Cyprus", *The Cyprus Review*, Volume 5, Fall 1993, Number 2,

Maria Hadjipavlou-Trigeorgis. "Different Relationships to the Land: Personal Narratives, Political Narratives, Political Implications and Future Possibilities in Cyprus" in *Cyprus and Its People*, V. Catolyh, Boulder, CO: Westview Press, 1998.

Charles Hess, *Culture, Technology, Communication: Towards an Intercultural Global Village*, Albany: State University of New York Press, 2001.

David Hitchcock, *U.S. Public Diplomacy,* Washington, D.C.: The Center for Strategic and International Studies, Volume X, Number 17.

Michelle LeBarron, *Bridging Troubled Waters: Conflict Resolution from the Heart*, San Francisco, CA.: Jossey-Bass Press, 2002.

Peter Kivisto, *21st Century Sociology: Multiculturalism in a Global Society*, Oxford: Blackwell Publishing, 2002.

John Paul Lederach. *Building Peace: Sustainable Reconciliation in Divided Societies*. Washington, D.C.: United States Institute of Peace Press, 1997.

Michael Pickering, *Stereotyping: The Politics of Representation*, New York: Palgrave Press, 2001.

Stuart Oskamp, ed., *Reducing Prejudice and Discrimination*, London: Lawrence Erlbaum Associates, 2000.

John Prendergrast and Emily Plumb, "Building Local Capacity: From Implementation to Peacebuilding" in *Ending Civil Wars by* Stephen Stedman, Donald Rotchild and Elizabeth Cousins, Lynne Rienner, 2002.

The United States Information Agency: A Commemoration, Published by the USIA, p.30.

Frank Webster, *Culture and Politics in the Information Age: A New Politics*, London: University of Oxford Press, 2001.

M. Yoshin, "The Role of Joint Narrative in Conflict Resolution: The Case of Cyprus" in *From Nationalism to Multiculturalism: The Literature of Cyprus, Greece, and Turkey,* by Maria Hadjipavlou-Trigeorgis, UK: Middlesex University Press, 2000.

Young Yun Kim, *Becoming Intercultural: An Integrative Theory of Communication and Cross-Cultural Adaptation*, London: Sage Publications, 2001.

William Zartman, J. Lewis Rasmussen, *Peacemaking in International Conflict: Methods and Techniques*, Washington, D.C.: United States Institute of Peace Press, 1997.

BBC News UK Edition, "Emotion as Cyprus border opens", http://news.bbc.co.uk/1/hi/world/europe/2969089.stm, April 23, 2003.

BBC News UK Edition "Cyprus trade ban lifted" http://news.bbc.co.uk/1/hi/world/europe/2989873.stm, April 30, 2003.

BBC News UK Edition "Country profile: Cyprus", http://news.bbc.co.uk/1/hi/world/europe/country_profiles/1016541.stm, Sunday, June 8, 2003.

INTERVIEWS

1/03 Nicos Anastasiou, Peace Leader and Citizen Diplomat

1/03 Daniel Hadjittofi, Director of the Fulbright Commission of Cyprus

1/03 Dr. Maria Hadjittofi, Professor of Conflict Resolution, University of Cyprus

2/03 Dr. Benjamin Broome, Professor of Communications, Arizona State University and Former US Fulbright Scholar to Cyprus

2/03 Dr. Sheryl Brown and Margarita Brown, Co-Directors of the Virtual Diplomacy Initiative (VDI), United States Institute of Peace

5/03 Diana Chigas, Former Director of Conflict Management Group's Conflict Resolution Training Program and Co-Director of the Cyprus Consortium, Professor of Conflict Resolution, Fletcher School of Law and Diplomacy

5/03 Dr. Hrach Gregorian, Director of World Affairs Institute

5/03 Turgut Durduran, Co-founder of Peace-Cyprus.org and Cyprus-Action.org

5/03 Eser Keskiner Co-founder of Peace-Cyprus.org and Cyprus-Action.org

5/03 Dr. Elizabeth Prodromou, Founder of the Cambridge Foundation for Peace and CyprusMediaNet.com, Assoc. Dir., Inst. on Religion & World Affairs, Asst. Prof. Dept. of Int'l Relations Boston University

5/03 Arthur Martirosyan, Director of the Momentum Project, Conflict Management Group

5/03 Dr. John Ungerleider, Director of CONTACT program and Professor of Conflict Resolution at the School of International Training, Former US Fulbright Scholar to Cyprus

5/03 Dr. Harry Anastasiou, Co-founder Tech4Peace.org, Professor of Conflict Resolution, Portland State University

6/03 Dr. Dimitris Apostolidis, Program Coordinator for CyprusMediaNet.com

6/03 Dr. Yiannis Laouris, Co-founder of Tech4Peace.org

Made in the USA
Charleston, SC
02 December 2014